INSIGHT GUIDES

MELBOURNE
smart guide

APA PUBLICATIONS

Part of the Langenscheidt Publishing Group

Contents

Areas

A–Z

Atlas

*Inside Front Cover:
    Melbourne Locator*
*Inside Back Cover:
    Around Melbourne*

Highlights

▲ **St Kilda** A beachside suburb returning to its glorious heyday with great cafés, restaurants, a safe beach and resident penguins.

▶ **Eureka Tower** With its 92 levels, this is Melbourne's tallest building. Its main attraction, Eureka Skydeck 88, is the Southern Hemisphere's highest viewing platform.

◀ **Royal Botanic Gardens** The city's green lung is the place to jog, stroll and enjoy nature.

▲ **Laneways** Melbourne's network of laneways exude a sense of intimacy and intrigue, as well as being home to many intimate restaurants, bars and shops.

▲ **Melbourne Zoo** See koalas, kangaroos and wombats in specially designed habitats.

◀ **Federation Square** An architectural marvel with open-air public space for people to meet up or relax.

Melbourne

Melbourne, located in the southeastern part of Australia, is the largest city in the state of Victoria. The official City of Melbourne consists of the city centre and inner-city suburbs, each with its own distinctive character. It has been consistently listed as one of the world's most liveable places. The air is fresh, the tree-lined streets are clean, and public transport efficient.

Melbourne Facts and Figures

Resident population: 93,105 (4 million in metropolitan area)
City of Melbourne area: 37.6 sq km (14½ sq miles)
Melbourne metropolitan area: 7,694 sq km (2,971 sq miles)
Conferred city status: 3 August 1849
Residents born overseas: 41.7 percent
Total workers employed in Melbourne: 413,136
Total area of parkland: 567.8 hectares (1,419½ acres)
Number of café/restaurant/bistro seats: 145,116
Demonym: **Melburnians**

PAST AND PRESENT

In 1835, Melbourne was founded by Tasmanian settlers – farmer John Batman and businessman John Pascoe Fawkner. The settlement became a town in 1842 and within several years was raised to the status of a city, whose growth and population swiftly escalated thanks to the gold rush between 1850s and 1860s.

The Melbourne of the 21st century is known for its unique characteristics, in particular the labyrinth of laneways and arcades; the extensive and efficient tram network; picturesque parks and gardens; and beautiful heritage buildings juxtaposed with cutting-edge architecture. Not forgetting the Yarra River that flows through.

ORIENTATION

The inner city covers an area radiating out approximately 7km (4 miles) from the Central Business District (CBD) and has a high population density, especially in the CBD and St Kilda. The CBD was designed in a grid pattern by surveyor Robert Hoddle in the 1830s, so the streets are very easy to navigate. Some inner-city suburbs can be accessed on foot from the CBD. Just to its north are the tree-lined streets of Carlton, as well as the bohemian shopping and entertainment streets of neighbouring Fitzroy. To get around, hop on a tram or take the City Loop train.

Across the Yarra River are the modern developments of Southbank and the green oasis of the Kings Domain and Royal Botanic Gardens. Further south are the high-end suburbs of South Melbourne, South Yarra and Toorak. Nearer to the bay is popular beachside suburb St Kilda, reached via trams, buses or trains.

Melbourne is positioned around Port Phillip Bay – separated from Bass Strait by the Bellarine Peninsula in the southwest and Mornington Peninsula in the southeast. Its surrounding regions include Yarra Valley and the Dandenong Ranges, the foothills of the Macedon and Great Dividing Ranges, and of course the world-famous Great Ocean Road that stretches from Torquay all the way to Warrnambool.

Below: Melbourne Museum's bright exterior.

Above: Melbourne's cityscape is known for its abundance of public art.

MELBOURNIANS

Melbourne is one of the most ethnically and culturally diverse cities in the world. Greater Melbourne's population is about 4 million (the second-largest urban population in Australia after Sydney – although this is predicted to change in the next couple of decades). Metropolitan Melbourne has the largest annual growth in Australia, knocking Sydney into second place. Based on current forecasts, the population of the City of Melbourne is predicted to hit 150,000 by 2030.

The multicultural population (nearly 42 percent were born abroad) lends further uniqueness to the city. There are 140 different cultures, derived from four main waves of migration since the city was founded. There were the indigenous Australians who were displaced by the European settlement in the 1830s, followed by the 1850s gold-rush influx of people from all over the world, including a substantial number of Chinese. This was followed by post-World War II European migrants, then post-1970s migration from Vietnam and Cambodia.

The largest migrant groups today arrive from the UK, Italy, Vietnam, China, New Zealand, Greece, India, Sri Lanka and Malaysia. Migrants from African nations such as Sudan and Ethiopia have been increasing too in recent years.

Australian culture is easygoing and friendly; you are likely to be greeted with a 'G'day mate' wherever you go. Sport is a favourite pastime in Melbourne, especially footy (Australian Rules), cricket, swimming and basketball. Locals are just as likely to flock to cultural events and festivals happening year-round, visit lively markets, have brunch in well-loved cafés or dinners in fine restaurants.

CLIMATE

Melbourne is well known for its 'four seasons in a day' weather conditions. The city has warm to hot summers, with an average of 26°C (79°F). January and February are the hottest months, and the maximum temperature can reach 40°C (104°F) and beyond on some days. In winter, the average maximum temperature is 14°C (57°F) and minimum 6°C (43°F), although the wind chill can make it seem much cooler. The best time to visit is in spring or autumn, when the temperature is pleasant.

The City Centre

The heart of Melbourne is where the action is, with everything on offer from top restaurants, bars and fabulous shopping, to theatre, art and a range of other cultural activities. In the City of Melbourne, which comprises this central area and the inner-city suburbs, the pace of life is less frenetic than Sydney, yet always abuzz with exciting festivals and events. It's hard to get lost here as Melbourne's centre is made out of grids, peppered with myriad laneways, all ideal for walking, the recommended way to get around. The tram lines are also efficient, as is the city train loop which allows you to hop on and off whenever you wish.

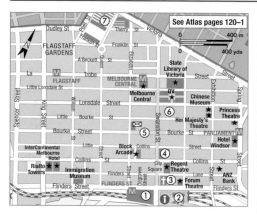

The **Forum Theatre**, not far from Federation Square, boasts unique neo-Gothic architecture adorned with gargoyles and Roman-esque statues as well as a blue-sky ceiling that forms the illusion of an open-air venue. This theatre has hosted live bands and comedy festivals over the years. SEE ALSO ARCHITECTURE, P.28, 29, 31; FILM, P.51; MUSEUMS AND GALLERIES, P.76, 77; THEATRE AND DANCE, P.104

COLLINS STREET

The ornate Gothic Revival architecture of ANZ 'Gothic' Bank often captivates curious passers-by. Visitors are welcome to take self-guided tours in the bank. An **ANZ Banking Museum** is housed on the lower ground floor, showcasing the story of Australia's banking heritage.

Rialto Towers was the first skyscraper with an observation deck until Eureka Skydeck took over the role with its shinier, taller tower and viewing platform. At the base of the tower is the **InterContinental Melbourne Hotel**, formerly the Rialto Hotel.

Parallel to the main thoroughfare of Collins Street

FLINDERS STREET

Flinders Street Station ①, at the corner of Flinders and Swanston Streets, is Melbourne's most famous landmark and meeting place. Across from the station is the narrow Degraves Street, lined with small eateries. It also links to the ultra-hip Flinders Lane, which is packed with great cafés and galleries.

Directly opposite the station is the sprawling **Federation Square** ②, a dedicated cultural precinct. Located here are the **Melbourne Visitor Centre**, the **Ian Potter Centre** featuring the **National Gallery of Victoria's Australian Art Collection**, **ACMI (Australian Centre for the Moving Image)**, **Champions – The Australian Racing Museum**, and a variety of restaurants. The irregularly shaped city square was considered an architectural marvel for Melbourne and planned as an 'integrated civic space'. It's often a hive of activity, with lively events being held.

Across from Federation Square is the historic **St Paul's Cathedral** ③, designed by English architect William Butterfield. Constructed in 1880, the 'Gothic Transitional' church building was restored a couple of years ago.

Left: Federation Square is always buzzing with activity.

Built in 1910, the gold-coloured grand station is the oldest in Australia; an earlier station on the same site was founded in 1854. It is also the busiest railway station in the Southern Hemisphere, with more than 110,000 passengers passing through on an average weekday.

is Little Collins Street, lined with boutiques and cafés. Located here is the 19th century Block Arcade, filled with mosaic-tiled flooring and with a wrought-iron and glass canopy. Here are the **Hopetoun Tea Rooms**, one of Melbourne's tea-time institutions.

At the corner or Swanston and Collins Street is **City Square**. Just opposite City Square is **Melbourne Town Hall** ④, a heritage-listed building dating from 1870. It plays an important role in Melbourne's cultural and civic activities.

The **Regent Theatre** has richly decorated interiors and stages major musical productions. Further down is the Paris End of Collins Street, lined with posh boutiques.

SEE ALSO ARCHITECTURE, P.30; CAFÉS, P.36; HOTELS, P.61; SHOPPING, P.98; THEATRE AND DANCE, P.105

SWANSTON AND BOURKE STREETS
Bourke Street Mall ⑤ is a pedestrian strip with a tram running along the centre. Here you will find major department stores **Myer** and **David Jones** and the historic **Royal Arcade**.

State Library of Victoria and its lush lawns is another landmark noted for its heritage architecture and history. Just a few steps away, **QV** is a major shopping spot where you can

Below: in Chinatown.

find a host of designer boutiques and lifestyle stores.

Chinatown ⑥ has a huge range of Chinese eateries and narrow laneways with small grocery stores or bars. After your yum cha feast, find out more about the history of Australia's Chinese culture at the **Chinese Museum**.

Nearby, **Melbourne Central** is a shopping and entertainment complex with an underground train station, part of the City Loop. Lonsdale Street is famous for its Greek eateries.

SEE ALSO ARCHITECTURE, P.30; MUSEUMS AND GALLERIES, P.76; SHOPPING, P.97, 99

CORNER OF ELIZABETH AND VICTORIA STREETS
Queen Victoria Market ⑦ is one of the city's most iconic attractions. Founded in 1878, the massive market is popular for its fresh foods and deli section.

SEE ALSO MARKETS, P.73

SPRING STREET
On Spring Street, you will find the **Princess Theatre**. Further down is the **Hotel Windsor**. Built in 1883, this is Australia's only independent 'grand hotel'. It is most famous for its traditional afternoon teas.

SEE ALSO HOTELS, P.61; THEATRE AND DANCE, P.105

East Melbourne

This elegant district is where one of the city's favourite green lungs, Fitzroy Gardens, is located. Within the gardens are charming attractions such as Captain Cook's Cottage, the Model Tudor Village and the *Fairies Tree*. The imposing St Patrick's Cathedral, which one can see even from a distance, welcomes visitors to soak in the solemn yet serene atmosphere. East of Fitzroy Gardens towards the inner suburb of Richmond is the renowned Melbourne Cricket Ground, more commonly known as MCG, a venue that has hosted many major sporting events, including the 1956 Melbourne Olympics.

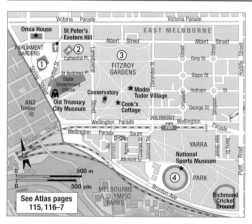

Above: the atmospheric St Patrick's Cathedral.

PARLIAMENT OF VICTORIA

The **Parliament House** ① is a landmark at the edge of the city centre. The building is surrounded by the triangular-shaped Parliament Gardens, the members-only Parliament House Garden, and the Gordon Reserve with a fountain sculpted by William Stanford, a trained stonemason who was imprisoned for robbery. Construction of the Parliament House began in 1855, but the grand structure with its sweeping steps was built in various stages from 1856 to 1929.

Those keen on politics are welcome to see Parliament in action when it is sitting. The Legislative Council and the Legislative Assembly also have public galleries.

ST PATRICK'S CATHEDRAL

The lofty Gothic Revival architecture of **St Patrick's Cathedral** ② was constructed in stages from 1858 to 1940. The mother church of the Catholic Archdiocese of Melbourne boasts striking interiors whose stunning stained glass produced in Munich and Birmingham have been carefully restored. Thanks to its excellent acoustics, it is a favoured venue for choral groups and musicians.

Dating from the 1840s, St Peter's Eastern Hill is an Anglican church just across the street from St Patrick's Cathedral. This pre-gold-rush church contains many fine artworks, including 19th- and 20th-century stained glass, a

Built in 1958, the Modernist Orica House (formerly the ICI House) near the Parliament House was the tallest building in Australia until 1961 (when the first tall building was completed in Sydney). It broke the height limit applied to all the city buildings then, which was only 11 to 12 storeys.

Left: explore Cook's Cottage in Fitzroy Gardens.

lectern by German wood-carver Robert Prenzell and bronzes by Hungarian Andor Mészáros.
SEE ALSO ARCHITECTURE, P.31

FITZROY GARDENS

Fitzroy Gardens ③ was named after Sir Charles Augustus Fitzroy, Governor of New South Wales (1846–51) and Governor-General of the Australian Colonies (1851–5).

One of the main highlights here is **Cook's Cottage**. Originally built in 1755 in Yorkshire, England, by Captain James Cook's parents, the house was shipped to Australia in 1933 and reconstructed. Step into the double-storey home and experience the Cooks' 18th-century lifestyle. Meanwhile, at the Discovery Centre, you can learn about the captain's life, tales of his voyages and his tragic death.

Fitzroy Gardens' **Conservatory** was established in 1930, dedicated to horticulture. The building was based on the Spanish Mission architectural style. There are five different floral displays over the year.

The *Fairies Tree*, completed in 1934 by Ola Cohn, is a work of art beautifully hand-carved onto the stump of a 300-year-old red gum tree, showcasing fairies, dwarfs and goblins, alongside koalas and other Australian animals.

Another highlight in the heart of the gardens is the quaint **Model Tudor Village** donated in 1948 to the City of Melbourne by artist Edgar Wilson. Representing a Kentish village in the Tudor period, it comprises thatched cottages, barns, a school, and a scale model of Shakespeare's home.
SEE ALSO PARKS AND GARDENS, P.86

MELBOURNE CRICKET GROUND

The **MCG** ④ was constructed in 1853 when the then 15-year-old Melbourne Cricket Club had to relocate from its former site because the railway track of Australia's first steam train was to be built across the oval. Since early days, the MCG has hosted major events such as the 1956 Olympic Games, the 1992 cricket World Cup final, international cricket games, and VFL/AFL Grand Finals. Aside from sporting events, the MCG has also housed music concerts and even a mass by Pope John Paul II during his visit in 1986. With the recent redevelopment of the stadium, the MCG can now sit 100,000 people. Sports fans can take an MCG Tour backstage to boot. The grounds also house the **National Sports Museum**, home to the Olympic Museum, Sport Australia Hall of Fame, Australian Cricket Hall and Melbourne Cricket Club Museum.
SEE ALSO SPORTS, P.102

Below: the statue of Dennis Lillee at the MCG.

Carlton and Fitzroy

Carlton is a diverse inner-city suburb where you will find attractions such as the Melbourne Museum, Royal Exhibition Building and Lygon Street, lovingly dubbed 'Little Italy', a favourite hangout of students from the prestigious University of Melbourne. The tourist-friendly Melbourne Zoo and the Old Melbourne Gaol are also located near this area. East of Carlton is the bohemian enclave of Fitzroy, where cafés, restaurants, bars and eclectic stores abound, particularly along Brunswick, Gertrude and Smith streets. There is never dull moment in this vibrant, edgy and trendy district.

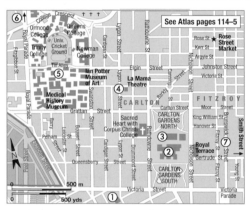

Above: Melbourne Museum has a striking design.

CARLTON

At the fringe of the city near Carlton is **Old Melbourne Gaol** ①. This 19th-century prison located at the end of Russell Street (between Victoria and La Trobe Streets) was in operation from 1842 to 1929. Many of Australia's notorious gangsters and infamous characters, including controversial bushranger and fugitive Ned Kelly, were jailed and hanged here. Visitors can experience the Watch House and be 'arrested' and 'locked up' in a site that hasn't changed much since the early 1900s. The Old Magistrates' Court is another area where visitors can experience standing in the dock or sitting in the judge's chair.

The World Heritage-listed **Royal Exhibition Building** ② set in the middle of the pretty Carlton Gardens is one of the oldest remaining exhibition pavilions in the world. Completed in 1880 for the first Melbourne International Exhibition, which attracted entries from 33 countries showcasing products of the Industrial Revolution, its beautifully restored interior and opulent dome are still as stunning as ever. Today it continues to host trade shows, food events and cultural fairs.

Just opposite Carlton Gardens is the **Melbourne Museum and IMAX Theatre** ③, with its striking, multi-coloured facade. Opened in 2000, the museum exhibits Victoria's

Many Italian migrants made Carlton their home in the early 1900s. Lygon Street became the precinct where Melbourne's café culture surfaced. In recent years, a new culture and events hub as well as public open space was introduced. The development of the Italian-inspired Argyle Square or Piazza Italia along this street is a joint project between the City of Melbourne and Milan. Many festivities are held here, lending even more life and colour to the area.

Left: Brunswick Street is an epicentre of boho culture.

Melbourne Zoo ⑥ houses koalas, kangaroos, wombats and many more uniquely Aussie creatures. Opened in 1862, the setting today has expanded to a variety of landscapes including lush 'African jungles' and 'Asian rainforests' to create fitting habitats for the many lions, tigers and exotic species. SEE ALSO CAFÉS, P.37; CHILDREN, P.40, 41; MUSEUMS AND GALLERIES, P.78; WILDLIFE, P.110

FITZROY

For the best of bohemian culture, visit **Brunswick Street** ⑦. This edgy, alternative and artistic stretch bursts with life throughout the day. Pop into one of the quirky vintage boutiques, art galleries or eclectic bookstores, followed by brunch at a small café or dinner and drinks.

Nearby is the **Rose Street Artists' Market**, which occupies the space of a former junkyard in the back-streets of Fitzroy. Open every weekend, this is Melbourne's first dedicated art and design market.

Down on Gertrude Street you will find more eateries, art galleries and specialist bookshops such as **Artisan Books** and **Books for Cooks**.

Smith Street, parallel to Brunswick Street, has a multicultural vibe and has many cheap Asian, Greek and Middle Eastern food options, plus local designer stores. Johnston Street is a Spanish quarter where you can enjoy tapas or drink at a flamenco bar. SEE ALSO LITERATURE, P.71; MARKETS, P.74; SHOPPING, P.96

history, culture and natural environment. Taking pride of place is the gigantic blue whale skeleton, a living temperate forest, Australia's most famous race horse, Phar Lap, a stimulating children's gallery designed for three- to eight-year-olds, and the Bunjilaka Aboriginal Cultural Centre, featuring Aboriginal art, artefacts and performances among

Below: in the Old Quad at Melbourne University.

other things. Movie buffs can experience 2D and 3D shows at IMAX's massive six-storey-high screen.

Within walking distance from Melbourne Museum is **Lygon Street** ④, also known as Little Italy. This historic heartland of the city's Italian community is lined with beautiful Victorian terraces, cake and gelato shops, and, of course, restaurants and alfresco cafés, many of which stay open until late at night.

On the west of the Lygon precinct is **Melbourne University** ⑤, a sprawling campus with beautiful architecture and quiet cloisters. Founded in 1853, it is the second-oldest university in Australia and the oldest in Victoria. It houses the **Ian Potter Museum of Art** – a leading university art museum displaying over 1,500 items from the campus's art collection.

Southbank, Docklands, South Wharf and South Melbourne

On the Yarra River's banks, the Southbank is home to Eureka Skydeck 88, the city's tallest viewing deck, and the artistic enclave comprising the National Gallery of Victoria and Arts Centre. Over in Docklands, the restaurants by the waterfront draw visitors, and heading southwards is South Melbourne Market, the city's oldest, which is very popular for its fresh foods.

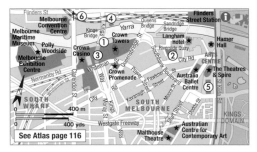

See Atlas page 116

SOUTHBANK

Southbank ① along Yarra River has a wide promenade, perfect for a stroll in the morning or evening to soak in the city's skyline.

Just opposite the **Langham Melbourne** hotel is **Eureka Skydeck 88** ②, the Southern Hemisphere's highest viewing platform. A lift zips you up to the 88th level, where you can view the entire skyline and beyond. If height is not a problem, step into 'The Edge', a glass cube that projects 3m (10ft) out from the building.

Within walking distance from the promenade is the **Crown Entertainment Complex** ③, anchored by the Crown Casino and three hotels. The complex also houses a host of outstanding restaurants such

as **Nobu** and **Maze**, top shops and entertainment.

Just across the river is **Melbourne Aquarium** ④, home to fascinating sea creatures including Australia's only King and Gentoo penguins from Antarctica.

In the heart of the leisure and entertainment precinct is the **Arts Centre** with its landmark spire. The Theatres Building and Hammer Hall (currently closed for

redevelopment until 2012) are part of the centre, which also houses over 200,000 performing arts items and memorabilia from artistes such as Kylie Minogue and Dame Edna Everage.

On Sunday over 150 stalls of Victoria's finest arts and crafts congregate at the **Arts Centre Sunday Market** to sell handmade ceramics and leather book covers, among others.

Art buffs will enjoy a visit to Australia's oldest public art gallery, the **National Gallery of Victoria** ⑤. From 1861, the gallery has showcased many masterpieces from Europe, including Picasso, Cézanne and Renoir. It will be celebrating its 150th birthday in 2011.

The nearby **Australian Centre for Contemporary Art** with its rusty steel structure is an architectural icon. It is the only major public art gallery in the country that places emphasis on commissioning rather than collection. In the area too is **Malthouse Theatre @ The CUB Malthouse**, dedicated to contemporary Australian theatre.

Left: a spire crowns Melbourne's Arts Centre.

Left: a fantastic view of the city from the Eureka Skydeck.

SOUTH MELBOURNE
South Melbourne Market
⑦, established in 1867, is Melbourne's oldest continuing market, popular for its fresh foods. Many people enjoy chilling out at the Cecil Street café stretch on a sunny day, where tables spill out onto the sidewalk.

Located between Port Phillip Bay and the city centre, **Albert Park** is a lovely parkland; it is also home to the Australian Formula One Grand Prix, held annually in March. The park's most popular attraction, though, is the **Melbourne Sports and Aquatic Centre**, with its Olympic-sized pools, diving facilities, wave pool and water slide.

SEE ALSO FESTIVALS AND EVENTS, P.48; MARKETS, P.75; PARKS AND GARDENS, P.86; SPORTS, P.101

DOCKLANDS
Southern Cross Station
⑥ is a major railway station and the most important transport hub serving the Victoria region.

Etihad Stadium is a major sporting and concert venue, the only football stadium in the Southern Hemisphere with a fully retractable roof. There are

---

Launched in 1997, Crown is the largest casino in the Southern Hemisphere, with 350 table games and 2,500 poker machines. On opening night, Australian actress Rachel Griffiths infamously showed up uninvited and topless as an anti-gambling protest.

---

tours to visit the AFL players' changing rooms and umpires' tunnels.

In the heart of Docklands is the Promenade, great for waterfront dining. There are also attractions such as the **National Ice Sports Centre**, a new world-class Olympic-sized ice sports and leisure venue. Not far from the waterfront is Harbour Town, boasting two levels of laneway shopping.
SEE ALSO SPORTS, P.102

SOUTH WHARF
Melbourne Convention and Exhibition Centre takes pride of place at the new South Wharf. It is the first and only '6 Star Green Star' environmentally rated convention centre in the world. The adjacent interactive **Melbourne Maritime Museum**'s highlight is the *Polly Woodside*, an iconic 1885 tall ship made in Belfast, Northern Ireland.

See Atlas pages 116, 118–9

Domain and Royal Botanic Gardens

Some of Melbourne's most visited attractions are located in this area. The magnificent Shrine of Remembrance is where people gather to remember Australians who sacrificed their lives during the World Wars. The lush Royal Botanic Gardens are a green oasis that appeals to nature-lovers with its picturesque lakes, gardens, flowers and sculptures. It's a favourite place for local joggers at weekends and perfect for a stroll, especially in spring and autumn's clement weather.

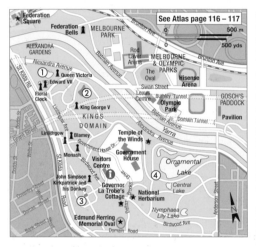

See Atlas page 116 – 117

Hollywood Bowl, this a popular venue for summer concerts as well as home to Carols by Candlelight. This iconic Melbournian event has been held on Christmas Eve every year since 1937. Contemporary and traditional perform-ances are featured during this celebration, attended by massive crowds, who come with their candles to the auditorium or sit on their blankets on the lawn encircling the venue.

An important landmark in Melbourne, the **Shrine of Remembrance** ③ was built between 1928 and 1934 as a memorial for the 114,000 Australians who served the British Empire and memorialises 19,000 of the people who sacrificed

QUEEN VICTORIA GARDENS

Queen Victoria Gardens ① is a well-manicured, triangular-shaped area just across the road from the National Gallery of Victoria. A highlight here is the well-known floral clock made of 7,000 vibrantly coloured plants that are changed twice a year. The clock was a present from a group of Swiss watch-makers to the city in 1966. The pretty garden is also adorned with ornamental ponds, sculptures and monuments to Queen Victoria and her son, King Edward VII.

SEE ALSO PARKS AND GARDENS, P.87

KINGS DOMAIN

Established in the mid-19th century, the sprawling Kings Domain surrounds the **Government House Reserve**, home of the Governors of Victoria since 1876, as well as the Sidney Myer Music Bowl and the Shrine of Remembrance.

Woven into the land-scape of the Kings Domain Park is **Sidney Myer Music Bowl** ②. Inspired by the

Left: the Shrine of Remembrance.

11am on 11 November 1918 marked the end of World War I. Originally called Armistice Day, it was renamed Remembrance Day after World War II. Every year at 11am on the 11th day of the 11th month, the city pauses to remember Australians who lost their lives during the wars.

are not only a place for recreation but also a vital resource for conservation, horticulture and education. Land was set aside for public gardens in 1846, but the design of the gardens was put together between 1879 and 1909 by the director William Guilfoyle. A huge variety of over 10,000 species of plants from around the world, including rare and threatened species, can be found here. There are three lakes in the garden too – Central Lake, Ornamental Lake and Nymphaea Lily Lake.

their lives during the Great War. The inspiration for the design by two former soldier architects and veterans of World War I, Phillip Hudson and James Wardrop, was the Mausoleum at Halicarnassus.

The shrine's sanctuary houses a black marble stone of remembrance with the words 'Greater Love Hath No Man'. On Remembrance Day, 11 November at 11am, a ray of sunlight shines through the roof's aperture to illuminate the inscribed word 'Love'. The eternal flame at the fore court was added in 1954 to commemorate those who served in World War II. Look out for the well-known bronze statue of *The Man with the Donkey*, representing John Simpson Kirkpatrick, who rescued wounded men at Gallipoli by carrying them away from the frontline on his donkey. Autumn is a lovely time to visit the surrounding Shrine Reserve, when trees change to different shades of orange, gold and red.
SEE ALSO FESTIVALS AND EVENTS, P.48

ROYAL BOTANIC GARDENS

The 160-year-old **Royal Botanic Gardens** ④

Some of the activities include an Aboriginal Heritage Walk with indigenous guides where visitors experience a traditional smoking ceremony plus learn about the traditional uses of plants for food, medicine and tools. The interactive **Ian Potter Foundation Children's Garden** is a hugely popular feature in the gardens. Kids can learn about natural produce such as interesting fruits, vegetables and herbs in the Kitchen Garden, or have fun and play hide and seek in the Bamboo Forest.
SEE ALSO CHILDREN, P.40; PARKS AND GARDENS, P.87

Left: the Sidney Myer Music Bowl, in King's Domain.

South Yarra, Prahran, Richmond and Toorak

South Yarra exudes an ultra-chic vibe thanks to Chapel Street. Lined with boutiques, it is a pleasant area to browse for the latest designs, window-shop or simply relax at a sidewalk café. Chapel Street links to Church Street in the north, towards the shopping district of Bridge Road in Richmond. Just east of South Yarra is Toorak, a posh suburb, home to the historic Como House and Park as well as Melbourne's affluent society. Southbound towards Prahran (pronounced P'Ran) is where the gay community gather for dancing.

Above: the Art Deco foyer of the Astor Theatre.

Bettina Liano have made their home here. Others to look out for include nobody, Australia's cult denim label, and Noir Desire for men and women. Aside from fashion, there are lifestyle stores and heaps of cool cafés, clubs and great restaurants.

The **Jam Factory** ② has an interesting history. From 1858 to 1876, the building housed the Victoria Brewery, becoming the 'Red Cross' preserving company from 1880 until 1895, when the new owner turned it into the OK Jam Co. It was later sold to Henry Jones, founder of the IXL brand. By the 1970s, due to a slowdown in demand, production of preserves and jam stopped completely. By the end of the decade, the Jam Factory shopping centre was opened. It now houses Village Cinemas, **Borders**, cafés and restaurants.

Prahran Market ③ on Commercial Road is one of Melbourne's favourite food markets. A central market was established in 1864 on the east side of Chapel Street, and was moved to Commercial Road in 1881. Ten years later, the new Prahran Market was opened, which is what we see today, apart from the portion that was gutted by fire in 1950. For more than a century, the market sold the freshest fruits, vegetables and meats. These days one can also find a host of gourmet deli foods, speciality and organic produce,

SOUTH YARRA AND PRAHRAN

Chapel Street ① is a shopaholic's dream, filled with upmarket boutiques and stores by cutting-edge local designers. Famous Aussie fashion labels such as **Alannah Hill**, **Collette Dinnigan**, **Metalicus** and

In World War I, a recruiting depot was established at the Prahran Town Hall for citizens to enrol for the war. Although there were many German watchmakers, jewellers and food merchants in the area, legislation was passed to prevent them from advertising or selling goods with German brand names.

See Atlas pages 117, 119

Left: the Jam Factory in Prahran.

Prahran Market's fruit and vegetable section was burnt down on Boxing Day 1950. Only the meat section and part of the front shops and facade were left intact. After the fire, a temporary replacement structure was built; it was only in 1972 that a new market was completed.

ent families; the Armytage family stayed at Como from the early 1900s until 1959, when they handed over the property to the National Trust. Visitors can follow a guided tour or explore at the own leisure the estate's vegetable garden and lawns. When the tour is over, enjoy afternoon tea at the site's Café Bursaria.

Those who want to venture eastwards will find Toorak Village, frequented by wealthy residents of the nearby suburbs of Toorak and South Yarra. The small 'village' has boutiques, books, supermarkets, florists and cafés.

wines, baked goods and, of course, cafés.

Besides the market, Commercial Road is also Melbourne's gay district. The **Market** and **Xchange** hotels are famous for their drag shows.

Chapel Street Bazaar at the corner of High Street and Chapel Street houses over 75 independent dealers displaying all manner

Below: shopping in a Toorak Village boutique.

of antiques, vintage and second-hand goods from Prince Charles and Lady Di mugs to old books, cushions and lace.

At the southern end of Chapel Street near Dandenong Road is the **Astor Theatre**, a grand 1930s cinema with charming Art Deco architecture. The sound system is state-of-the-art.

SEE ALSO FASHION, P.46; FILM, P.51; GAY AND LESBIAN, P.56; MARKETS, P.72; SHOPPING, P.99

TOORAK

Not far from Chapel Street is the **Como Historic House and Garden** ④. The beautiful gardens and historic mansion were built by Edward Eyre, one of Australia's richest pioneer families. The house was constructed in 1847 from bricks made using Yarra River mud. Como was sold and bought over by differ-

RICHMOND

Bridge Road is famous as a shopping enclave, in particular clothing factory outlets that sell reasonably priced goods. It is also a classified heritage area. For a sense of history, look at the bronze plaques displayed on the buildings. **Richmond Town Hall** is where you can find cultural information on Bridge Road. When your shopping spree is over, head to nearby Victoria Street, lined with great Vietnamese eateries, to munch on freshly made rice paper rolls or slurp up bowls of beef pho.

17

St Kilda

S t Kilda is one of the most popular beachside destinations that's not too far from the city centre. It has shed its shady past of the 1960s and 1970s, and is bringing back the glory days of the early 20th century. In those days, this bayside surburb was a playground for the well-heeled who built their mansions on St Kilda Hill. Soon after the tramlines reached the suburb in 1888, less affluent Melburnians flocked here at weekends. Today St Kilda has transformed into a fashionable spot with hip live music venues, stylish apartments, popular beachside restaurants, and excellent cake shops and cafés.

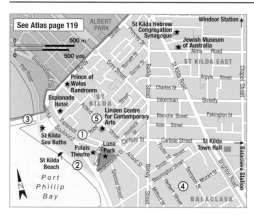

Above: decorative plate at the Jewish Museum of Australia.

UPPER ESPLANADE

The **Upper Esplanade** ① stretch affords lovely views of Port Phillip Bay and features an arts and crafts market on Sundays. Opened in 1878, the **Esplanade Hotel** has been the place to enjoy live music gigs for more than a century. It continues to showcase bands and DJs across three stages every evening.

SEE ALSO MARKETS, P.72; MUSIC, P.83

LOWER ESPLANADE

The **Lower Esplanade** ② is home to **Donovans** and **Stokehouse**, a couple of well-loved beachside res-taurants set in beautifully restored 1920s houses. Opposite the restaurants is the historic **Luna Park** fun-fair with its iconic laughing face and rollercoaster which have been classified by the National Trust. Families still come here with kids in tow for the various rides.

Next to Luna Park is the **Palais Theatre**, a major concert venue that show-cases live music, Australian bands, famous interna-tional performers such as Harry Connick Jr, Cindi Lauper and Duran Duran, comedy events and many others. It is considered the largest theatre in Australia, and proudly shows off its fine Art Deco architecture. In recent years, the theatre has reintroduced a full-scale ballet and the **St Kilda Film Festival**.

Further up the stretch is the well-restored 19th-century **St Kilda Sea Baths**, now a complex with restaurants, bars, a day spa featuring purified sea water, an indoor sea-water pool and a gym.

SEE ALSO RESTAURANTS, P.94

ST KILDA BEACH

The wide, sandy and safe **St Kilda Beach** is one of the most popular beaches on Port Phillip Bay, for swimming and a variety of recreational activities.

If you head to the beach in the evenings, you will

Left: the entrance to Luna Park on the Lower Esplanade.

famous fluffy kooglhoupf cake. Backpackers, tourists and locals love hanging out at the cafés here. Located in a Victorian mansion here is the **Linden Centre for Contemporary Arts**, a not-for-profit contemporary art gallery. At the corner of Fitzroy and Acland Streets is the **Prince Bandroom**, a live music haunt for six decades, that has hosted many top musicians such as Coldplay, Pink and Lenny Kravitz.

SEE ALSO CAFÉS, P.39; MUSIC, P.83

ST KILDA EAST

Founded in 1982 at South Yarra's synagogue of the Melbourne Hebrew Congregation, the **Jewish Museum of Australia** moved to Alma Road in 1992. One of the exhibits in the permanent collection is the Australian Jewish History Gallery – showcasing the contribution of Jewish migrants in Australia over the last 200 years. It is opposite one of Melbourne's most beautiful synagogues, the **St Kilda Hebrew Congregation Synagogue**, which offers guided tours.

The earliest maps, dating from *c.*1865 showed that the area that Luna Park currently occupies was a wasteland mostly covered by a lagoon which was eventually drained in the 1870s. At the end of 1906, 'Dreamland', an outdoor amusement park sitting in the area where Luna Park is today, was launched. Although Dreamland didn't last long and was demolished due to lack of visitors, it had many attractions, including an old-style wooden rollercoaster which remained until World War I.

and strolls. Many Melburnians enjoy cycling and fishing here too. The pier, including its old shed and pavilion, has been around since the 1850s. The iconic Edwardian-style St Kilda Pier Kiosk, constructed in 1904, was sadly burnt down in 2003 by an arsonist. Due to popular demand, the kiosk was rebuilt in 2005 based on original drawings, and has resumed serving snacks and drinks.

ACLAND STREET

St Kilda Botanic Gardens ④, located on Blessington Street (off Acland Street), has palm-lined paths, a lovely rose garden and shady lawns, great for a respite away from the buzz at the beach

Acland Street ⑤ is most popular for its celebrated cake shops, in particular **Monarch**, which sells its

be able to spot numerous penguins returning home after a day of fishing. The little creatures live in the St Kilda Breakwater, which was built for the 1956 Olympic Games to provide a safe harbour for yachts.

St Kilda Pier ③ is a favourite for panoramic views of the city, sunsets

Below: on Acland Street.

Around the Bay

Port Phillip Bay has many townships with their own distinct charm. It's all about breathtaking water views, plus a fair bit more. Williamstown's historic maritime village atmosphere has always appealed to Melburnians, who love to visit at weekends. Southbound around the edge of the bay are the renowned bathing boxes of Brighton, seen on many postcards and paintings. Even further down the curve of the bay is Mornington Peninsula, whose top-rated wineries, old lighthouses, imposing cliffs, beaches and many other attractions make this part of Victoria very much sought after as a place to live.

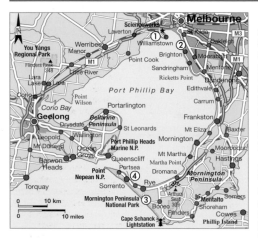

Located in **Spotswood**, not far from Williamstown, **Scienceworks** presents science and technology in an interactive format with live demonstrations, special activities and guided tours. Meanwhile, the **Melbourne Planetarium** offers digital simulations of outer space. SEE ALSO CHILDREN, P.41; MUSEUMS AND GALLERIES, P.80

BRIGHTON BEACH

The upscale suburb of **Brighton**, 13km (8 miles) south of the city, has several long, sandy beaches including Middle Brighton, Brighton and Dendy Street. In the late 19th century this was a favourite seaside destination.

Dendy Street Beach's famous colourful **Brighton Bathing Boxes** ② are

WILLIAMSTOWN

Flanking the serene Hobson's Bay, **Williamstown** ① is a historic maritime suburb just 15 minutes by car from Melbourne City. The place's charm is mostly contributed by the grand 19th-century buildings. Many early settlers decided to make Williamstown their home thanks to the sheltered harbour.

Walk down Williamstown jetty and soak in the views of the bay and city. Anchored here is HMAS *Castlemaine*, an Australian World War II minesweeper. The restored warship show-

casing nautical exhibits and memorabilia is open to the public every weekend.

At Nelson Place, Williamstown's business heart in the early days, there is a bevy of cafés and restaurants as well as shops and galleries. A craft market is held in Commonwealth Reserve on Nelson Place every third Sunday of the month. Point Gellibrand, right at the end of Nelson Place, is where the original Williamstown Lighthouse stands. Built in 1840, it is thought to be the first harbour light of its kind in the country.

The first settlers of what would become the colony of Victoria arrived by sailing ship in 1835 from Van Diemen's Land (the original name used by early European settlers for Tasmania). In 1837, the newborn settlement was divided into two towns: Melbourne, named after the British prime minister of the time, Lord Melbourne, and Williamstown, after King William IV.

Left: the famous Brighton Bathing Boxes.

boast three cottages which used to be residences of the lighthouse keepers. Stroll down the boardwalk to enjoy stunning ocean views in the morning, and sit on the lawn at night and stare at the starry sky. The historic lighthouse built in the 1800s is still operating and open daily for tours.

Although not as famous as Yarra Valley, Mornington Peninsula's boutique wineries, about 50 of them, are equally beautiful and produce top-quality wines, in particular Pinot Noir and Chardonnay. They range from small award-winning wineries like **Ten Minutes by Tractor** to famous ones like **Montalto**, which has a great restaurant and outdoor sculpture gallery.

Sorrento ④ is famous for its beaches and 1860s grand homes and hotels made of local limestone. The Sorrento Pier is where a ferry operates from every day of the year – taking passengers and vehicles across to Queenscliff and the Great Ocean Road. Right at the tip of Mornington Peninsula is Point Nepean National Park.

SEE ALSO VINEYARDS, P.109

set against a backdrop of the city skyline. These 82 quaint structures are an iconic part of Port Phillip Bay and remain as they did over a century ago. The huts, relatively uniform in scale and proportion, have timber framing and corrugated iron roofs. Owned and maintained by licensees, who are members of the Brighton Bathing Box Association, they have made their huts a unique work of art by painting them with a riot of colours.

Brighton's foreshore offers barbecue facilities, windsurfing, yachting and boating amenities. Visitors can take a scenic walk via Green Point from Brighton Beach Railway Station.

MORNINGTON PENINSULA

Mornington Peninsula National Park ③ is a favourite summer destina-

> In the 1860s, there were between 100 and 200 bathing boxes in Brighton. Unlike the ones we see today which are built near the cliffs, the 'boxes' were originally positioned near the water's edge; many were washed away by storms.

tion for Melburnians. From native bushland of Greens Bush inland to basalt cliffs at Cape Schanck on the coast, nature-lovers can enjoy the best of both worlds. For a panoramic view, head inland and up a windy road to **Arthurs Seat**, whose lookout affords spectacular views, including of the city skyline, the You Yangs and Mount Macedon.

The **Cape Schanck Lightstation** is reminiscent of one of those lighthouses featured in Enid Blyton's *Famous Five* stories. The sweeping grounds here

Below: in Mornington Peninsula National Park.

21

Yarra Valley and Dandenong Ranges

Yarra Valley, a wine region barely an hour's drive from Melbourne, is a favourite destination for a wine-tasting session, a satisfying meal or simply a breather. This cool-climate wine region has a rich, 150-year history in viticulture and winemaking, and several award-winning estates, some with restaurants overlooking lovely landscape. Meanwhile over in Dandenong Ranges it's all about nature, forests, flowers, plus charming villages with small shops, galleries and Devonshire teas.

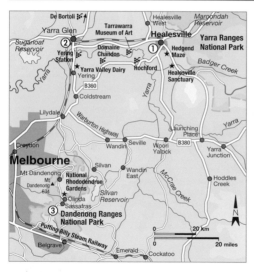

Above: a cuddly-looking koala at Healesville Sanctuary.

HEALESVILLE

Healesville ① in the foothills of the Great Dividing Range is touted as a regional food and wine hub, with many cellar doors open to the public for tastings and sometimes tours. Among the many vineyards in Yarra Valley, a renowned one in the Coldstream area is **Rochford**, known for producing top-quality wines. There is an elevated art gallery where guests can muse over renowned Australian artworks. The estate also holds many exciting concerts and festivals. In the area too is **Domaine Chandon**, founded in 1986 by the world-renowned French champagne house Moët & Chandon. The beautifully restored 1910 **Healesville Hotel**'s restaurant, the **Dining Room**, offers fresh regional produce.

Gastronomy aside, visitors can meet native animals in their natural habitat at **Healesville Sanctuary**, a bushland reserve home to more than 200 species of indigenous birds, mammals and retiles.

To get an overview of the surrounding Yarra Valley, hop on the Heritage Railway Ride from Healesville Station for a 40-minute return trip.

SEE ALSO CHILDREN, P.40; RESTAURANTS, P.95; VINEYARDS, P.108; WILDLIFE, P.110

Victoria's first vineyard was planted at Yering Station in 1838 by the Scottish-born Ryrie brothers, who moved their cattle southwards from Sydney to Yarra Valley. In the early 1900s, the Yarra Valley wine industry was in decline, but started to flourish again in the 1970s when demand for Victoria's cool-climate wines increased.

Left: vineyards in the Yarra Valley.

National Rhododendron Gardens which boast 15,000 rhododendrons as well as a plethora of beautiful azaleas, camellias and daffodils. Walk around the garden and enjoy views of Silvan Reservoir Park and the blue Australian Alps.

A popular attraction is **Puffing Billy**, Australia's oldest steam train, dating from the early 1900s. It is still chugging away on its original mountain track from Belgrave to Gembrook. The train operated from 1900 until 1953 when a landslide blocked the track; it was closed a year later due to operating losses.

Located a short drive from Puffing Billy is the charming **Olinda Village**, where you can shop for art and crafts and antiques.

The Devonshire cream tea at the themed **Miss Marple's Tea Room**, in the village of **Sassafras**, is a popular attraction and treat.

On the top of Mount Dandenong is **SkyHigh**, its viewing platform and bistro affording sweeping views of the area and beyond (Mornington Peninsula and Port Phillip Bay), as well as the city lights in the distance.

SEE ALSO CHILDREN, P.41; CAFÉS, P.39

YARRA GLEN

In **Yarra Glen** ②, Victoria's first vineyard was originally planted in 1838. The estate has a restaurant and art gallery sitting on landscaped gardens. One of the most popular farmers' markets in this region, the **Yarra Valley Regional Food Group's Farmers' Market**, is held every third Sunday of the month in the historic barn of Yering Station.

SEE ALSO MARKETS, P.75;

THE DANDENONGS

The sprawling **Dandenong Ranges National Park** ③ covers the Sherbrooke Forest, Doongalla Reserve, Ferntree Gully National Park, Olinda State Forest and Mount Evelyn Forest. This is the protected habitat of species such as the ground-dwelling lyrebirds.

The park is well known for its mountain ash forests, the world's tallest flowering plant. Situated on a hilltop are the

Below: a Furphy water tank at Yarra Glen's Gulf Station.

For a different vantage point over the verdant valley, book a hot-air balloon tour by Balloon Sunrise, an exciting 'mode of transport' to soak in the surroundings. The journey begins at Balgownie Estate, 4km (2½ miles) north of the Yarra Glen township. After the flight, guests get to enjoy a champagne breakfast at the winery's restaurant.

23

Great Ocean Road

Many people are familiar with the 12 Apostles attraction along the Great Ocean Road, in southwest Victoria, but there are many more gems along this winding coastal stretch. They include tranquil towns like Lorne and Apollo Bay, the Otway National Park for its gorgeous waterfalls, and Warrnambool, a favourite spot for whale-watching. To explore this long and dramatic coastline, you will need at least a couple of days. Deemed one of the world's most scenic drives, the road was built as a memorial to soldiers who lost their lives in World War I. The drive from Melbourne takes about three to four hours. Look out for koalas feeding on gum-tree leaves along the way.

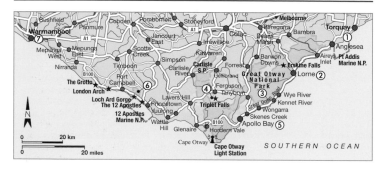

TORQUAY TO APOLLO BAY

The Great Ocean Road officially starts at **Torquay**, Australia's surf capital. Located here is Surfworld, the world's largest surfing museum, which showcases the Australian Surfing Hall of Fame. Between Torquay and Anglesea is the renowned **Bells Beach** ①, a long stretch that lures many world-class surfers to the Rip Curl Pro, the oldest professional surfing competition in the world. **Anglesea**, about 15 minutes' drive away, is surrounded by national parkland and known for its wide front beach, sheer cliffs and coastal heathland.

Lorne ② is the most popular holiday spot on the Great Ocean Road. Its picnic and barbecue facilities and golden sand appeal to many families and beachgoers. The main stretch of Mountjoy Parade has many cafés where you can refuel.

Another major attraction is the **Great Otway National Park** ③, a lush temperate rainforest filled with endemic flora and fauna. It is home to several stunning waterfalls, including the tall and slender Erskine Falls, just a short drive inland from Lorne, as well as the majestic Triplet Falls, recently redeveloped to provide new and unique views of the cascades. Walks to the different waterfalls vary in lengths and levels of difficulty.

Otway Fly Tree Top Walk ④ is the longest and highest (600m/1,968ft long and 25m/82ft) high) walk of its kind in the world. Suspended high in the forest, near the Triplet Falls, the Otway Fly was designed to have minimal impact on the beech myrtle forest environment. The tallest point is the viewing platform of the spiral tower at a heart-pounding height of 45m (148ft).

> Constructed between 1919 and 1932, the Great Ocean Road was built by 3,000 ex-servicemen who had returned to Australia after World War I. In those days, their only digging tools were picks, shovels and horse-drawn carts. The 243km (151-mile) road carved out of rock, bushland and forest was created as a memorial to the men who died fighting in the conflict.

Left: Bells Beach in Torquay is a surfing hotspot.

tragic accident on 1 June 1878, when about 50 people died after the *Loch Ard* ship smashed into Muttonbird Island's cliffs in stormy weather, just days after completing a three-month voyage from England to Melbourne. It was this gorge and its small beach that were the lifesavers for the two survivors, apprentice crewman Tom Pearce and young passenger Eva Carmichael. Visitors to Loch Ard today can descend the staircase to the beach and cave where Tom and Eva struggled to survive.

At the western end of the Great Ocean Road is the historic city of **Warrnambool** ⑦, which became an important port during the Victorian Gold Rush and burgeoned in the 1850s. Located on the Shipwreck Coast, this area boasts pristine beaches, old lighthouses, manicured gardens and green parks.

Overlooking Lady Bay is Flagstaff Hill, a fascinating recreated maritime village of the early Port of Warrnambool. Discover more about the past by checking out the display of relics from shipwrecks found along the Shipwreck Coast. Presented at dusk every day is the 'Shipwrecked' Sound and Laser Spectacular show.

Warrnambool is also a whale nursery, because many whales come here to give birth annually. **Logans Beach**, which has a viewing platform, is the best location to see Southern right whales between June and September, when they migrate to this area.

APOLLO BAY TO WARRNAMBOOL

Midway along Great Ocean Road is the beautiful **Apollo Bay** ⑤, nestled at the foothills of the Otway Ranges. There are great restaurants and cafés to dine at, as well as a Saturday market. Nearby is Cape Otway, which offers amazing walks along some of Victoria's highest ocean cliffs. The Cape Otway Light Station, perched on one of the imposing cliffs, is the oldest surviving lighthouse in the country. Since 1848, its light has guided many ships safely.

Drive towards the west for another 50 minutes and you will soon arrive at the **Port Campbell National Park** ⑥, where the world-famous **12 Apostles** stand majestically in the ocean. Over 20 million years, the forces of nature gradually eroded Port Campbell's

limestone cliffs, forming caves and eventually arches. When they crumbled, rock islands were left standing in the waters.

This process also created along this coastline other beautiful natural formations such as London Arch (formerly called London Bridge until part of the 'bridge' collapsed) and Loch Ard Gorge, so named for a

Below: the recreated inn in Flagstaff Hill, Warrnambool.

A–Z

In the following section Melbourne's attractions and services are organised by theme, under alphabetical headings. Items that link to another theme are cross-referenced. All sights that are plotted on the atlas section at the end of the book are given a page number and grid reference.

ALTO HOTEL
ON COLLINS

Architecture

Much of inner-city Melbourne's architecture is Victorian in style. The grand buildings of this era were built with gold-rush money, and a walk down Collins Street in the CBD gives you a great example of such architecture. The National Trust of Australia (Victoria) (www.nattrust.com. au) has been actively working to preserve the unique character of Melbourne's streets, declaring many of them Urban Conservation Areas. Additionally, other architecture styles such as Art Deco, Postmodern and Romanesque can also be seen around the city. The following listings cover a sample of the city's architectural highlights.

EUREKA TOWER

Riverside Quay, Southbank; www.eurekaskydeck.com. au; train: Flinders Street; map p.121 D4

Melbourne's tallest building is an architectural icon. It's named after the Eureka Stockade rebellion during the Victorian gold rush in 1854, and the crown of the building is gold in colour, with a red stripe, representing the gold and the bloodshed. Also, the blue facade with white lines is intended to represent the blue and white flag of the stockade. Officially opened in 2006, the building consists of 91 floors (plus one underground), with 84 floors of apartments. The facade is made of glass and aluminium panels. Eureka Sky Deck 88 was opened in May 2007, with 30 viewfinders and an observation terrace.

FEDERATION SQUARE

Corner of Swanston and Flinders Streets, City Centre; www.fedsquare.com; train: Flinders Street; map p.121 D3

Above: Flinders Street Railway Station.

In 1996, an international design competition was announced for the development of this new civic precinct. The winning architecture studio believed their design reflected the true spirit of federation – independent identities combining to form a larger whole. Federation Square was officially opened in 2002 and touted as a public space for gatherings and so on.

The building facade system allows for the individual buildings to be differentiated from each other, while simultaneously maintaining an overall coherence. There are nine separate cultural and commercial buildings in total. Sandstone, zinc and glass were used as cladding materials, within a modular basis established by the triangular pinwheel grid. The open-air plaza is covered in cobblestones of Kimberley sandstone, to distinguish this surface from the city's existing pavement. Different shades of stones, including reds, oranges, yellows, pinks, purples, mauves and greys, are arranged to create a pattern across the plaza's surface.

SEE ALSO MUSEUMS AND GALLERIES, P.76, 77

FLINDERS STREET RAILWAY STATION

Corner of Flinders and Swanston Streets, City Centre; tel: 03-9610 7476; train: Flinders Street; map p.121 D3

This grand Edwardian building that spans more than a city block has adorned scores of postcards of Melbourne. It is also the talking –

Left: Victorian terrace houses on Powlett Street.

is topped by a jewelled copper dome. It's also an Arabic-inspired building, with minarets, a clock tower, oriel windows and cupola. Inside is a sky-blue ceiling decorated with small stars, mimicking a twilight sky, and giving an 'outdoor' feel.

SEE ALSO THEATRE AND DANCE, P.104

MELBOURNE'S GPO

350 Bourke Street, City Centre; tel: 03-9663 0066; www.mel bournesgpo.com; Mon–Thur 10am–6pm, Fri 10am–8pm, Sat 10am–6pm, Sun 11am–5pm; train: Melbourne Central; map p.121 C2

Designed in neo-Renaissance style, Melbourne's GPO is one of the city's most important public buildings. A two-level building was built between 1859 and 1867, and in 1887 a third level was added, as well as the famous clock tower. The building was redesigned in 1919 by American architect Walter Burley Griffin. It was only in 1992 that the building's postal role ended, and a planning permit for a shopping mall on the site was granted the next year. But this permit eventually lapsed, as did another one in 1997. The building opened as a retail centre in 2004. The ceiling was restored, but the modern design retains many of the heritage aspects of the site. There are now over 50 stores spread over three floors, with a diverse mix of dining, shopping and event spaces.

SEE ALSO SHOPPING, P.99

Victorian terrace homes are an interesting find in Melbourne – the city has one of the best collections in the world. Cast iron was used in the popular Victorian Filigree style during the 1880s, while the polychrome brick style produced a uniquely Melbourne style of terrace. Multi-storey terrace housing also became prevalent in some suburbs, but little of it remains. That found in suburbs such as Albert Park, Fitzroy and Carlton is subject to strict heritage overlays, to preserve it.

and meeting – point for residents and visitors. The architecture has been described as 'French Renaissance' and is, in fact, strongly influenced by the French architecture of the 1900s. It also uses some Art Nouveau motifs, present in the leadlight windows and in some of the ironwork. The building was completed in 1910 and designed by railway architect James Fawcett in partnership with railway engineer H.P.C. Ashworth,

after the design was selected through an architectural competition held in 1899. The most striking features of its golden-yellow facade are the clock tower, the domes and the grand arohwayo.

FORUM THEATRE

154 Flinders Street, City Centre; tel: 03-9299 9860; www. forummelbourne.com.au; train: Flinders Street; map p.121 D3

Built in 1928 and formerly known as the State Theatre, this building was built in the neo-Gothic style and

Below: the ornate, neo-Gothic Forum Theatre

Above: in the State Library of Victoria.

PARLIAMENT OF VICTORIA

Spring Street, East Melbourne; tel: 03-9651 8911; www.parliament.vic.gov.au; train: Parliament; map p.121 E1

One of Melbourne's best-known landmarks, the building is everything you would expect of a Parliament House – sweeping steps, grand colonnade and elegant lamps. It is, however, an incomplete building. Work began on the two legislative chambers in 1856 and was finished in just 10 months. The two chambers were joined at the rear by the Library, which was completed in 1860, and formed a U-shaped building. From 1877 to 1879, the Grand Hall (now the Queen's Hall) was built, as was the Vestibule, which gave a formal entry to the building. The West Facade and Colonnade were completed in 1888, while the entrance steps and laps were added between 1888 and 1892. 1893 saw the partial completion of the North Wing, which is in effect a basement level. And, in 1929, the Northeast Wing was constructed, as a refreshment room.

RIALTO TOWERS

525 Collins Street, City Centre; tel: 03-9614 5888; www.rialto.com.au; train: Southern Cross; map p.120 B3

Rialto Towers is sheathed entirely in blue reflective glass and stands tall and proud as a modern icon amongst its Victorian-style neighbours.

Officially opened in 1986, Rialto is one of the tallest reinforced concrete structures in the Southern Hemisphere. Two buildings are linked here – the South Tower has 55 lettable floors (63 floors in total), while the North Tower has 40 (43 floors in total).

STATE LIBRARY OF VICTORIA

328 Swanston Street, City Centre; tel: 03-8664 7000; www.slv.vic.gov.au; train: Melbourne Central; map p.121 C1

Joseph Reed won a competition in 1853 for his Roman Revival design,

Southern Cross Station (Spencer Street, Melbourne; tel: 03-9619 2579; www.southerncrossstation.net.au) is another iconic station building. Rebuilt in 2006 – and formerly known as Spencer Street station – it has a unique roof design that naturally extracts internal air and fumes from the station, without the use of any electric fans. It's open and transparent, thanks to the external envelope of expansive glass facades.

Below: the Gothic Revival spires of St Patrick's Cathedral are a city landmark.

Right: St Paul's Cathedral from the Eureka Skydeck.

and construction started soon after. The official opening took place in February 1856, but it wasn't until 1859 and 1864 that the South and North Wings were completed, respectively. The grand portico – made of Tasmanian freestone – was added in 1870 and the large central dome was added in 1913.

A statue of Sir Redmond Barry, the founder of the State Library of Victoria, welcomes visitors from his position in the middle of the steps. A statue of Lieutenant-Governor Charles La Trobe, another founder of the Library, sits at the north end of the lawn. The entire State Library of Victoria is composed of 23 buildings plus the grassed area at the front, which has been there since the 1930s and is a popular spot for people to relax.

ST PATRICK'S CATHEDRAL

Corner of Gisborne Street and Cathedral Place, East Melbourne; tel: 03-9662 2233; www.stpatrickscathedral.org. au; train: Parliament; map p.121 E1

Construction on this grand Gothic Revival Church finished in 1897 and is

Some buildings in Melbourne are protected by law, and are listed on the Victorian Heritage Register (VHR). Examples are Young & Jackson Hotel and the State Library of Victoria (both on Swanston Street), St Kilda Town Hall in St Kilda and the Treasury Building in East Melbourne.

said to be architect W.W. Wardell's masterpiece. The spires are a prominent city landmark and the Gothic arch is a highlight of the church. The archway has a bronze tracery grill, featuring St Patrick, with St Brigid and St Columba on each side.

ST PAUL'S CATHEDRAL

Corner of Swanston and Flinders Streets, City Centre; www.stpaulscathedral.org. au; train: Flinders Street; map p.121 D3

Designed by distinguished English architect William Butterfield, the architectural style of this cathedral is described as Gothic Transitional, being a combination of Early English and Decorated. After some problems with

Butterfield – he refused to visit Melbourne – the building was completed under the supervision of Joseph Reed, and it was consecrated in 1891. There have been works done to the cathedral since then, such as the erection of the spires in 1926, extensive works on the exterior in the 1960s and a major National Trust appeal to enable the restoration of its magnificent organ. More recently, restoration works were done to the interior and exterior in 2009.

Outside on the lawn is a statue of Captain Mathew Flinders, who mapped the coast of Australia in 1801 to 1803 and was the first cartographer to use the term 'Australia' on maps.

31

Bars and Pubs

Melbourne has a vibrant bar scene; a particularly popular staple is the series of stylish drinking dens located in obscure laneways throughout the CBD. Many of these venues are to be found behind anonymous doorways and attract punters through a mixture of word of mouth and discreet advertising. In the inner-city suburbs, there are entertainment strips such as Brunswick, Gertrude and Chapel Streets, full of hip bars and pubs. Many of these places are small and intimate, perfect for chilling out with friends. *See also Music, p.82, and Nightlife, p.84.*

THE CITY CENTRE
Bar Lourinha
37 Little Collins Street; tel: 03-9663 7890; www.barlour inha.com.au; Mon–Thur noon–11pm, Fri noon–1am, Sat 4pm–1am; tram: 112; map p.121 E2
Perch on a bar stool and work through the Iberian-style tapas menu, then complement the dishes with the Mediterranean wine list. Lively noise levels and interesting wine keep the mood jolly.

Croft Institute
21 Croft Alley; tel: 03-9671 4399; www.thecroftinstitute. com.au; Mon–Thur 5pm until late, Fri 5pm–3am, Sat 8pm–3pm; tram: 1, 3, 6 to Little Bourke Street; map p.121 D2
Croft Alley is one of those dark lanes you would think twice before walking down, but once you get there you will understand the venue's cool factor. This dim space in Chinatown is designed like a mad scientist's lab whose shelves are lined with old test tubes, beakers and other chemistry

Above: Madame Brussels' terrace has great views.

apparatus. Elbow your way through the crowds later in the night get or there early to score a seat. Check out the gym-turned-dancefloor at the top level.

Gin Palace
10 Russell Place; tel: 03-9654 0533; www.ginpalace.com.au; daily 4pm–3am; tram: 96 to Bourke Street; map p.121 D2
The seductive strains of lounge music and sound of cocktail shakers getting a workout greet you on entering this Melbourne institution. Its velvet-upholstered lounge chairs

are claimed by a pre-dominantly 30-something crowd, who are devoted to the bar's expertly con-cocted Martinis.

Golden Monkey
389 Lonsdale Street; tel: 03-9602 2055; www.golden monkey.com.au; Mon–Fri 5pm–late, Sat 7pm–late; tram: 19; map p.120 C2
You will find this trendy Asian-themed basement bar fashioned like an 'opium den'. A huge range of cocktails are served alongside Asian-style bar snacks. There is also lane-way seating if you wish to people-watch and soak in Hardware Lane's vibe at night.

Madame Brussels
Level 3, 59–63 Bourke Street; tel: 03-9662 2775; www.mad amebrussels.com; daily noon–1am; tram: 96; map p.121 D2
Astroturf and garden furniture inside, a huge balcony with skyscraper views outside, and good wine and cocktails to keep you happy.

Most of Melbourne's favourite bars are tucked away in laneways. Some are hard to find but worth all the effort. Some have nondescript entrances, with no signage. But that's only part of the fun. Just bring a map along or, even better, a local friend.

Melbourne Supper Club

Level 1, 161 Spring Street; tel: 03-9654 6300; Sun–Mon 8pm–4am, Tue–Thur 5pm–4am, Fri 5pm–6am, Sat 8pm–6am; train: Parliament; map p.121 D1

Walk through a nondescript wooden door and up a narrow flight of stairs to get to one of Melbourne's signature bars, just next to the Princess Theatre. The wine list is extensive and the cocktails and suppers excellent. Sink into one of the large armchairs and enjoy views of the Parliament House and the gardens.

Meyers Place Bar

20 Meyers Place; tel: 9650 8609; Mon–Thur 4pm–2am, Fri–Sat 4pm–4am; train: Parliament; map p.121 D2

One of the first laneway bars in Melbourne, Meyers Place was started by a group of architects who wanted a place where they and their boho friends could enjoy a quiet drink after work. Near Parliament House, it has been joined in the lane by the equally popular **Loop** (23 Meyers Place; tel: 9654 0500; www.looponline.com. au; daily 3pm–late).
SEE ALSO LANEWAYS, P.69

Misty

3–5 Hosier Lane; tel: 03-9663 9202; www.mistymelbourne.

Below: in the stylish hangout, Meyers Place Bar.

Left: find Misty down a funky laneway.

com; Tue 5pm–11pm, Wed 5pm–midnight, Thur 5pm–1am, Fri 5pm–3am, Sat 6pm–3am; train: Flinders Street; map p.121 D3

Down a laneway near Federation Square, the decade-old Misty keeps its cool with good beer, great tunes and a fashionably friendly attitude.

Money Order Office (M.O.O.)

Basement, 318 Little Bourke Street; tel: 03-9639 3020; www.moneyorderoffice.com. au; Tue–Sat 5pm–late; tram: 96; map p.121 C2

This plush basement bar and restaurant is set in the Money Order Office built in 1890 as an extension to the GPO. The dimly lit space is adorned with antiques and artefacts scoured from around the world. Take your pick from the 900 wines and pair them with the scrumptious bar-grazing menu.

New Gold Mountain

Levels 1 and 2, 21 Liverpool Street; tel: 03-9650 8859; www.newgoldmountain.org; Mon–Thur, Sat 6pm–late, Fri 5pm–late, Sun 8pm–late; train: Parliament; map p.121 D2

Another one of the city's popular bars located in an obscure venue with no noticeable signage. Walk up the narrow stairs and find dark, cosy alcoves adorned with red lanterns and old-school oriental furnishings.

Seamstress

113 Lonsdale Street; tel: 03-9663 6363; www.seam stress.com.au; Mon–Sat 5pm–late; tram: 19; map p.121 D1

There are many fabulous bars attached to restaurants, which are great for pre-and post-meals. Some of these include Little Press Club and Cellar, The Society and Longrain.

The restaurant and two bars (one on the ground floor and one on the top floor) are as stylish as they come and have quickly endeared themselves to the city's barflies. The owners know their wine and cocktails, and match these with a tempting array of bar snacks, including freshly shucked oysters, venison and shiitake mushroom spring rolls and char-grilled beef skewers.

Three Below

3 City Square, Swanston Street; tel: 03-9662 9555; www.threebelow.com.au; Sun–Wed noon–1am, Thur–Sat noon–3am; train: Flinders Street; map p.121 D3

An atmospheric concrete-and-timber cave at the back of the City Square, Three Below mixes under-stated cool with seasonal cocktails, fine wines and tapas. Don't miss the famous steak sandwich.

Transit Cocktail Garden

Level 2, Transport Hotel, Federation Square; tel: 03-9654 8808; www.transporthotel.com; Wed–Fri 5pm–late, Sat–Sun 5pm–late; train: Flinders Street; map p.121 D3

Perched above Taxi Dining Room, this late-night supper club has an outdoor terrace with amazing views of the city skyline, a lengthy wine list and live entertainment. At the ground level is the **Transport Public Bar** (tel: 03-9654 8808; daily 11am–late), with river views and a huge range of beer.

Young & Jackson Hotel

Corner of Flinders and Swanston Streets, Melbourne; tel: 03- 9650 3884; www.youngandjacksons.com.au; Mon–Thur 10am–midnight, Fri 10am–3am, Sat 9am–3am, Sun 9am–midnight; train: Flinders Street; map p.121 D3

One of Melbourne's oldest pubs, Young & Jackson has been quenching thirsts since 1861. Sip Australian micro-brewed beer and enjoy live entertainment at the main bar, or relax with tapas and wine at Chloe's Bar, where the famous *Chloe* nude portrait has been housed since 1909.

CARLTON AND FITZROY

Builders Arms

211 Gertrude Street, Fitzroy; tel: 03-9419 0818; daily 5pm–1am; tram: 112, 86; map p.115 E3

A sleek renovation has turned a former rough house into a fashionable nightspot with a good range of house wines, great pub food and a flashy decor. There is also a beer garden for larger groups.

Enoteca Vino Bar

920 Lygon Street, Carlton North; tel: 03-9389 7070; www.enoteca.com.au; Tue–Sat 9am–10pm, Sun 9am–4pm; tram: 1, 8

Combining a charming restaurant with a brilliant Italian produce and wine store, Enoteca Vino Bar is a source of all things quality and Italian. The bar offers over 400 wines and a good selection by the glass.

Little Creatures Dining Hall

222 Brunswick Street, Brunswick; tel: 03-9417 5500; www.littlecreatures.com.au; tram: 112; map p.115 E2

A massive industrial-style space with a pub, dining and retail concept under one roof. The Fremantle-based brewery presents a range of beers and pub grub such as pizzas and pies.

Little Markov

350–352 Drummond Street, Carlton; tel: 03-9347 7113; www.markov.com.au; Mon–Sat 5pm–late; tram: 1, 8; map p.115 D2

Cool, hidden bar in a former

Left: Young & Jackson Hotel has a long history.

Right: come for a cosy vibe at George Lane Bar.

bottle shop offers decent food, great drinks, old and new world wines, and a moodily lit atmosphere.

SOUTHBANK, DOCKLANDS, SOUTH WHARF AND SOUTH MELBOURNE

Bear Brass
Shop 3a, River Level, Southgate, Southbank; tel: 03-9682 3799; bearbrass.com.au; Mon–Fri 8am–late, Sat–Sun 9am–late; train: Flinders Street; map p.121 D4
Lively riverside bar with great views of the city, plenty of room, plus a good Aussie wine list and classic cocktails. On Thursdays, 2-for-1 cocktails are offered from 5pm.

Belgian Beer Café Bluestone
557 St Kilda Road, Melbourne; tel: 03-9529 2899; www.belgianbeercafemelbourne.com; daily 11am–late; tram: 16; map p.117 D4
Sit indoors in the historic bluestone building or outside under coloured lights in one of Melbourne's best beer gardens. The extensive range of Belgian beers, beer-friendly dishes, mussels with frites and waffles appeal to all. Barbecues are organised too.

Lamaro's
273–279 Cecil Street, South Melbourne; tel: 03-9690 3737 Mon–Sat noon–1am, Sun noon–11pm; www.lamaros.com.au; tram: 112; map p.116 B4
A beautifully renovated casual chic pub on a quiet leafy street offering eight beers on tap, imported and artisan bottled beers,

house cocktails and 12 single malt whiskies alongside great gastropub fare with Asian and Italian influence

SOUTH YARRA, PRAHRAN, RICHMOND AND TOORAK

Book Bar
67 Green Street, Windsor; tel: 03-9529 7899; www.backbar.com.au; Tue–Sun 5pm–late; train: Windsor, tram: 78, 79; map p.117 E2
This bar reminiscent of a glamorous 1940s residence has two lounges, red and gold, richly decorated with plush furnishings, lamps and paintings. Sit by the fireplace in winter, sip a glass of wine and soak in the intimate atmosphere.

Der Raum
438 Church Street, Richmond; tel: 03-9428 0055; www.derraum.com.au; daily 5pm–1am; tram: 79; map p.117 E1
At the 'Third Best Bar in the World', clued-in bartenders source for seasonal produce and specialist liquors to concoct their phenomenal molecular cocktails.

A huge range of drink bottles are suspended from the ceiling at the hip bar counter, which is one of the best spots to watch the bartenders concoct your sophisticated drinks with serious precision.

ST KILDA

Circa Bar
2 Acland Street; tel: 03-9536 1122; www.circa.com.au; daily 5pm–late; tram: 16, 96; map p.119 C3
Circa Bar at the Prince Hotel is deck out with communal tables and intimate nooks – a perfect place to chill out, sip wines and delight in freshly shucked oysters.

George Lane Bar
1 George Lane (off Grey Street); tel: 03-9593 8884; www.georgelanebar.com.au; Wed–Fri 6pm–1am, Sat–Sun 7pm–1am; tram: 16, 96; map p.119 D2
Cosy, intimate bar with good wine, spirits and cocktails. Drinks with interesting names like 'arrrgh me nuts' and 'slappy pappy' will draw your attention.

Cafés

Melbourne's café scene buzzes with baristas brewing cup after cup of coffee for connoisseurs, not to mention what often seems like half the city's population seeking their caffeine fix. Thanks to its significant Italian community, Melbourne's cafés probably offer some of the best coffees outside of Italy. Their espresso machines work overtime every day, and an arresting aroma of roasted beans wafts through the narrow laneways early in the morning when workers head to their offices, and continues through to the late afternoon. Understandably, these cafés are at the centre of the city's life.

THE CITY CENTRE

Breadwell

135 Flinders Lane; tel: 03-9650 8544; Mon–Fri 7am–5pm; train: Flinders Street; map p.121 D2

Good, honest, home-made fare (not surprisingly, they do bread well), served on vintage tableware in a buzzy, cluttered and slightly eccentric environment. There is a tempting variety of cakes and pastries displayed too.

SEE ALSO LANEWAYS, P.69

Hopetoun Tea Rooms

Shops 1 and 2, 282 Collins Street; tel: 03-9650 2777; www.hopetountearooms.com.au; Mon–Sat 8am–5pm, Sun 9am–5pm; train: Flinders Street; tram: 112; map p.121 C3

Sipping tea and tucking into scones at this 1891 tea room is a charming affair. Daily high tea from 10am to 3pm, priced at A$45 per person, is perfect for ladies who lunch, and anyone else who fancies tucking into savoury bites, petits fours and fresh season fruits. The scones with jam are the highlights.

Above: in the delightful Hopetoun Tea Rooms.

Journal Canteen

Shop 1 Level 1, 253 Flinders Lane; tel: 03-9650 4399; Mon–Wed 7am–6pm, Thur–Fri 7am–11pm, Sat 8am–6pm; train: Flinders Street; map p 121 D3

Pick up a magazine and relax in the sofa area or mingle with the crowd at the centre communal table flanked by overhead bookshelves. The menu serves crisp salads, fresh breads and rolls as well as scrumptious blackboard specials such as home-made meatballs with tomatoes and pilaf.

Laurent

306 Little Collins Street; tel: 03-9654 1011; www.laurent.com.au; Mon–Sat 8am–6pm, Sun 9am–5pm; train: Flinders Street; map p.121 C2

Housed in an old bank with a sweeping spiral staircase in the middle, Laurent is a favourite catch-up venue for many. The beautifully made cakes, petits fours, tarts, croissants and other sweet treats are displayed on the long counter.

Mr Tulk

State Library of Victoria, 328 Swanston Street (enter from La Trobe Street); tel: 03-8660 5700; www.mrtulk.com.au; Mon–Thur 7am–5pm, Fri 7am–9pm, Sat 9am–4pm; train: Melbourne Central, tram: 1, 3, 5; map p.121 C1

Named after the first librarian, Augustus Tulk, this airy, light-filled café is a great hangout spot after a visit to the historic library. Enjoy brunches, lunch dishes, fabulous desserts or drinks on Friday evenings. The menu offers gluten-free and vegetarian dishes too.

Left: Mario's is a classic Italian café.

Brunetti

194–204 Faraday Street, Carlton; tel: 03-9347 2801; Sun–Thur 6am–11pm, Fri–Sat 6am–midnight; tram: 1, 8; map p.115 D2

A sizeable café, gelateria and creperia that churns out delicious Italian cakes and biscuits alongside delicious savoury fare. The café only uses 100 percent Arabica roasted Vittoria coffee, so you are assured of top-quality stuff. Alternatively, try the unique Italian hot chocolate *(cioccolato caldo con panna)* – a secret family recipe. Brunetti also has another branch at City Square (214 Flinders Lane; tel: 03-9663 8085; Mon–Thur 7am–7pm, Fri 7am–midnight, Sat 8am–midnight, Sun 8am–7pm) next to St Paul's Cathedral. This outdoor spot is an excellent place to unwind and people-watch

Mario's

303 Brunswick Street, Fitzroy; 03-9417 3343; daily 7am–11pm; tram: 96, 112; map p.115 E1

Another crowd favourite, this fuss-free café with superb food and professional yet friendly service has drawn crowds since it was established in 1986. Start with an antipasto, followed by one of the 10 pastas in the menu. The home-made parpadelle with ragout and gnocchi are boldly flavoured and must-tries. Mario's is also a lovely spot for brunch.

Small Block

130 Lygon Street, Brunswick East; tel: 03-9381 2244; Mon–Fri 7.30am–5pm, Sat–Sun

---

Lovingly brewed Italian coffee is so favoured in Melbourne that popular coffee chain Starbucks has lost much of its lustre – and closed down many of its outlets and laid off a large number of staff. Lygon Street coffee shop owners in particular never welcomed this American brand into their precinct, which has since shut down its outlet there.

Pelligrini's

66 Bourke Street; tel: 03-9662 1885; daily 11am–11.30pm; train: Parliament; map p.121 D2

This tiny yet timeless espresso bar has been serving up coffees and hearty home-cooked pastas since 1954. It seems that the decor hasn't changed for decades, but no one is complaining. They are merely here for the unpretentious and generously portioned nosh.

CARLTON AND FITZROY

Breitzoz

Corner of Gertrude and Brunswick Streets, Fitzroy; tel: 03-9415 7588; www.breizoz.

com.au; Mon–Fri 12pm–3pm, Mon–Sat 6pm–10pm, Sat–Sun noon–5pm; tram: 96, 112; map p.115 E3

This well-loved crêperie is so French that you can just imagine dining in a little joint in Brittany. The menu features a huge list of savoury crêpes with ingredients like ham, cheese and mushrooms, and sweet crêpes with chestnut, chocolate, apple and many others. There are also the 'Les Crêpes Flambées', pancakes livened up with a dash of liqueur.

Below: find traditional decor and food at Pelligrini's.

8.30am–5pm; tram: 1, 8; map p.115 D2

This hip crowd-puller in Carlton serves superb all-day breakfasts and lunch dishes. Sit on the red vinyl chairs and tuck into corn fritters, panini and other simple but delicious fare.

SOUTHBANK, DOCKLANDS, SOUTH WHARF AND SOUTH MELBOURNE
Café Zappa

206 Bank Street, South Melbourne; tel: 03-9699 9333; www.zappa.com.au; Mon–Fri 7am–3.30pm, Sat 8am–3pm; light rail: 96; tram: 109, 112; map p.116 B3

Another spot that serves an all-day breakfast and honest home-style Italian-style dishes cooked from the heart. Not forgetting great Italian coffee.

Mart 130

107a Canterbury Road; Middle Park; tel: 03-9690 8831; daily 7.30am–5pm; tram: 96, 112, 130; map p.118 B1

Located in a former railway building next to a tram stop (number 130), this charming café overlooking Albert Park has some of the best breakfast dishes in town. Its signature dish is the oven-roasted corn fritters made of fresh corn.

DOMAIN AND ROYAL BOTANIC GARDENS
Observatory Café

Royal Botanic Gardens, Birdwood Avenue, South Yarra; tel: 03-9650 5600; www.observatorycafe.com.au; daily 7am–5pm; tram: 8; free Melbourne City Tourist Shuttle; map p.116 C2

Set amongst the 19th-century Observatory buildings and next to the Royal Botanic Gardens visitors centre, good coffee, all-day breakfasts and simply cooked café food make this a perfect pit-stop pre- or post-stroll through the park.

SOUTH YARRA, PRAHRAN, RICHMOND AND TOORAK
Café Greco

560 Chapel Street, South Yarra; tel: 03-9826 2888; www.cafegreco.com.au; daily 9am–late; train: South Yarra; tram: 8; map p.117 E3

For over 15 years Café Greco has been a constant crowd-puller, serving generously portioned Mediterranean-style dishes and excellent coffee. The array of cakes offered is heavenly – think Tim Tam or Mars Bar Cheesecake.

Richmond Hill Café & Larder

48–50 Bridge Road, Richmond; tel: 613-9421 2808; www.rhcl.com.au; tram: 75, 48

Housed in an airy 19th-century Victorian building, this cosy café is so popular for brunch that you'll have to book beforehand. Some favourites include Baghdad eggs – which is eggs fried with lemon and garlic, sprinkled with cumin and mint – as well as buttermilk pancakes with pure Canadian maple syrup. After your meal, check out the Larder's local and imported cheeses and gourmet products.

ST KILDA
Greasy Joe's

64–66 Acland Street; tel: 03-9525 3755; www.greasyjoes.com.au; Mon–Fri 11am–late, Tue–Thur 4pm–late, Sat–Sun 9am–late; tram: 16, 96; map p.119 D3

Well known for its generous all-day breakfast menu and massive burgers. Those with huge appetites can sink their teeth into 'The Fat Bastard', composed of triple beef, triple cheese, triple bacon, grilled onion, mayo and mustard – certainly not for the faint-hearted. To chill out, there is a courtyard garden bar and a pool room.

> Melburnians are so serious about their coffee that many barista training short courses are offered in various institutions in town. Coffee buffs get to join sessions such as 'coffee masterclasses', 'palate training' and 'milk texturing and coffee art'.

Right: relaxing at Richmond Hill Café & Larder.

Right: delectable treats at Monarch Cake Shop.

Il Fornaio
2 Acland Street; tel: 03-9534 2922; www.ilfornaio.net.au; Mon–Fri 7am–11pm, Sat–Sun 8am–11pm (closed 5pm–6pm); tram: 16, 96; map p.119 C3

This split-level warehouse space is a popular café and bakery during the day and at night becomes a smart local Italian trattoria serving hearty, restorative food. Pastry chef Philippa Sibley creates delicious pies, pineapple dough-nuts, lemon muffins and other sweet treats worth every calorie.

Monarch Cake Shop
103 Acland Street; tel: 03-9534 2972; www.monarchcakes. com.au; daily 7.30am–9pm; tram: 16, 96; map p.119 D4

The business was estab-lished by a Polish émigré in 1934 on Lygon Street who relocated it to St Kilda about four years later, and was eventually bought over by current owner Gideon Markham in 1996. The best-seller here is the rich chocolate kogl-houpf, a large ring-shaped cake made according to the shop's original recipe. Grab a table by the side-walk and tuck into some good old-fashioned cakes with coffee.

AROUND THE BAY
Red Hill Baker
Shop 5, Red Hill; tel: 03-5989 2733; daily 7.30am–6pm; hire a car

This bakery in Mornington Peninsula uses traditional baking methods (on a stone oven floor) for its sourdoughs, ciabatta and unique wine bread. There are wood-fired pizzas (on Friday and Saturday nights and Sunday lunch), as well as gourmet pies and home-made cakes to be had.

YARRA VALLEY AND DANDENONG RANGES
Miss Marple's Tea Rooms
382 Mt Dandenong Tourist Road, Sassafras; tel: 03-9755 1610; www.missmarples. com.au; daily 11am–4.30pm; hire a car

Besides its famous Devon-shire scones, decadent ice cream sundae and sticky toffee pudding, this quaint café also rustles up hearty cottage pie, quiche Lor-raine, Pimlico pastie and sandwiches.

Yarra Valley Dairy
McMeikans Road, Yerin; tel: 03-9739 1222; www.yvd.com. au; daily 10.30am–5pm (closed Christmas Day); hire a car

This cheese shop with a small café is located in a 100-year-old milking shed with beautiful views of Yarra Valley. Order a cheese plat-ter served with crispy pitta bread and cherry chutney, or have your caffeine fix. Perhaps enjoy a decadent home-made ice cream before leaving.

GREAT OCEAN ROAD
Kafe Kaos
54–56 Mountjoy Parade, Lorne; tel: 03-5289 2639; www.kafekaos.com.au; daily 7.30am–5.30pm (winter 8am–5pm); hire a car

This usually crowded spot serves the area's best pancakes – called the Pancake Stack, it comes with fresh fruit maple syrup and ice cream. The sub-stantial all-day breakfast menu includes the 'famous breakie foccacia', and lunch items include bur-gers, wraps and panini.

La Bimba
125 Great Ocean Road, Apollo Bay; tel: 03-5237 7411; daily 8am–3.30pm, 6pm–10pm; hire a car

Water views, a bohemian sense of style and a friendly attitude keep La Bimba popular with tour-ists and locals. The menu offers Modern Australian cuisine with influences from the Middle East and Asia, plus heaps of sea-food items.

39

Children

There are heaps of attractions in Melbourne and its surroundings to keep both kids and parents happy. The city is pleasantly family-friendly, with parents' rooms located in most shopping malls and tourist attractions. There are also many parks and gardens in the city centre itself, ideal for walks or picnics with the kids. Or visit one of the many nearby wildlife sanctuaries to learn more about Australia's distinctive animals. Meanwhile, if you want to keep your children entertained with cultural or educational activities, there are plenty of museums with purpose-designed spaces.

COLLINGWOOD CHILDREN'S FARM

18 St Heliers Street, Abbotsford; tel: 03-9417 5806; www. farm.org.au; daily 9am–5pm; charge; train: Victoria Park
Located on the banks of the Yarra River, this has a lovely setting for special monthly events that include Family Day (first Sunday) and farmers' market (second Saturday). Help milk the cow every day at 10am and 4pm.

HEALESVILLE SANCTUARY

Badger Creek Road, Healesville; tel: 03-5957 2800; www.zoo. org.au/HealesvilleSanctuary; daily 9am–5pm; charge, children under four free; train: Lilydale, then bus: 685, 686 to Healesville
Get up close and personal with Australia's native wildlife. The Sanctuary includes the Australian Wildlife Health Centre, for a behind-the-scenes look at the treatment of injured and orphaned animals. Animals include the dingo, koala, kangaroo and Tasmanian devil.
SEE ALSO WILDLIFE, P.110

Above: a raptor display at Healesville Sanctuary.

THE IAN POTTER FOUNDATION CHILDREN'S GARDEN

Royal Botanic Gardens, Birdwood Avenue, South Yarra; tel: 03-9252 2300; www.rbg.vic. gov.au; Wed–Sun 10am–sunset, daily 10am–sunset during Victorian State School holidays, 10am–sunset all public holidays, closed for eight weeks over winter; free; tram: 8; Melbourne City Tourist Shuttle; map p.117 C2
Play hide-and-seek in the plant tunnels, get close to the creepy crawlies in the natural pond, or get your hands dirty in the Children's Kitchen Garden.
SEE ALSO PARKS AND GARDENS, P.87

MELBOURNE AQUARIUM

Corner of King and Flinders Streets, City Centre; tel: 03-9923 5999; www.melbourneaquarium. com.au; daily 9.30am–6pm, 1–26 Jan 9.30am–9pm (last admission one hour before closing); charge; train: Flinders Street or Southern Cross; map p.120 C4
There are various worlds and experiences to be witnessed here. Come face to face with creatures such as penguins, sharks, seahorses and sea dragons.
SEE ALSO WILDLIFE, P.110

MELBOURNE MUSEUM

11 Nicholson Street, Carlton; tel: 13 11 02; http://museumvictoria.com.au/melbourne museum; daily 10am–5pm; charge, children 3–16 years free; train: Parliament; tram: Melbourne City Tourist Shuttle; map p.115 D2
The museum has a Children's Gallery aimed at three- to eight-year-olds. Within it is the Big Box exhibition gallery, which houses 1, 2, 3, Grow, where the story of growth among plants, humans and animals is explored. The IMAX

Left: get close up to sea life at Melbourne Aquarium.

check website for details; charge; train: Belgrave
This historic steam train is a genuine relic. It's 100 years old and still runs on its original mountain track from Belgrave to Gembrook in the Dandenong Ranges. Check the website for times, depending on where you want to join and alight.

SCIENCEWORKS AND MELBOURNE PLANETARIUM

2 Booker Street, Spotswood; tel: 13 11 02; museumvictoria. com.au/scienceworks; daily 10am–4.30pm (closed Good Friday and Christmas Day); charge, children 3–16 years free; train: Spotswood
Hands-on interactive exhibits here change every few months. The aim is to present science and technology in unexpected and involving ways. Learn all about the science behind how your muscles work at Sportsworks, or simply explore Nitty Gritty Super City, an exhibition designed for three to eight-year-olds. Young astronomers will be thrilled by the Melbourne Planetarium.
SEE ALSO MUSEUMS AND GALLERIES, P.80

> If you are looking for family-friend places to dine at, log on to **www.heybambini. com.au**, which lists baby and child-friendly restaurants in Melbourne and the surrounding areas. Whether you are in the city or heading out to the suburbs, this is the perfect place to find a stress-free dining option.

theatre also screens plenty of family-friendly films.
SEE ALSO MUSEUMS AND GALLERIES, P.78

MELBOURNE ZOO

Elliott Avenue, Parkville; tel: 03-9285 9300; www.zoo.org. au/MelbourneZoo; daily 9am–5pm; charge, children under four free; train: Royal Park
See animals from all over the world here, including the orangutan, red panda and Sumatran tiger. Take a photo with a kangaroo, tortoise or meerkat in the Animal Photo Experience or go behind the scenes with the keeper and enjoy a training session with the lions in the Lion Encounter.
SEE ALSO WILDLIFE, P.110

PENGUIN PARADE ON PHILLIP ISLAND

1019 Ventnor Road, Summerlands, Victoria 3922; tel: 03-5951 2830; www.penguins. org.au; open 10am, closing times vary; charge
A 90-minute drive from Melbourne takes you to the popular Penguin Parade on Phillip Island. At sunset, little penguins come out of the sea and waddle along the shore to their burrows.

PUFFING BILLY

1 Old Monbulk Road, Belgrave; tel: 03-9757 0700; www.puffing billy.com.au; from 10.30am,

Below: many unusual animals are housed at Melbourne Zoo.

SOVEREIGN HILL

Bradshaw Street, Ballarat; tel: 03-5337 1100; www. sovereignhill.com.au; daily 9am–5pm (until 5.30pm during daylight savings); charge; train: Ballarat
The gold-rush theme park allows you to pan for real gold. Just a 90-minute drive from Melbourne, it's a whole different world, with old-style shops and even a sound-and-light show.

Environment

Melbourne is a city that is trying its best to do something good for the environment. Recycling is popular and, while water restrictions are in place, the latter encourages people to save this precious natural resource. Getting around Melbourne is relatively stress-free; traffic jams are not that common, and air pollution tends to sit at good levels. The weather is possibly be the biggest problem here, with bushfires all too common in summer – on various scales – and very strong winds and storms often cause damage, usually during the winter months.

AIR POLLUTION

Compared to other similar urban centres internationally, Melbourne's air quality is relatively good and has certainly improved since the 1980s. Environment Protection Authority Victoria (www.epa.vic.gov.au) was set up to protect, care for and improve the state's environment. The main contributing factor to pollutants here are motor vehicles, responsible for about half of the pollution in summer.

Above: Melbourne is seeking ways to reduce traffic snarls.

TRAFFIC CONGESTION

Melbourne has more roads and freeways per capita than comparable cities. VicRoads (www.vicroads.vic.gov.au) is the authority in charge of the state's roads and highways. Traffic can get pretty heavy on highways during peak hours, and ways of reducing traffic have been under debate in the past few years. There are several websites where you can check what the traffic is like, with regular updates.

These include the Vic-Roads site, www.racv.com.au, and victoria.snarl.com.au.

FLOODING

Storms do occur in Melbourne, but the city's drainage system copes well with most heavy rain. During the occasional intense storm, not all of the water is able to get down the drains quickly enough, resulting in floods. Some parts of Victoria are more prone to flooding, but these are generally more country areas and places that sit very close to rivers. The Bureau of Meteorology issues flood warnings throughout Australia, and Melbourne Water operates a 24-hour rainfall and river level monitoring network.

BUSHFIRES

Bushfires are common in summer, but usually in country areas of Victoria, where there is a lot of bushland. Saturday, 7 February 2009 – Black Saturday – saw the worst bushfires in Australian history and has been classed as the country's greatest natural disaster. In summer, fire restrictions are often issued and, during days of extreme heat, total fire bans are declared. This means that nobody in the area where the ban is declared can light a fire. The Country Fire Authority (www.cfa.vic.gov.au) issues such warnings.

CLIMATE

Melbourne has a temperate climate. Summers are

Left: keep an eye on the sky: Melbourne's weather is notoriously changeable.

occur sometimes too, usually in January or February.

RECYCLING

Melbourne has a big tradition of recycling, and every house is given a recycling bin, which is cleared once in two weeks. Melburnians are encouraged to recycle their trash, and most of them abide by these rules. National Recycling Week (recyclingweek. planetark.org) takes place across the country, usually in November.

PLASTIC BAGS

Plastic bags are given out in most supermarkets and stores, although customers are encouraged to bring their own environmentally friendly shopping bags or buy one from the shops. It is common to see shoppers lugging their own 'green' bags, especially at supermarkets.

WATER

There are water restrictions in place in Melbourne. Following years of drought, the country's water catchment areas haven't received the best supply of water, and such restrictions have been in force for a few years now. Depending on the stage of the restrictions, they disallow actions like washing your car at home, watering your plants daily and using sprinkler systems. The use of water tanks is encouraged, as is using recycled water for tasks like watering the plants. Water-saving devices such as showerheads and toilets are encouraged too.

Australia is doing its best to reduce its carbon footprint. Walk To Work Day (www.walk.com.au) is one such initiative. Apart from the obvious health benefits, it also encourages people to trim their carbon footprint.

---

warm to hot and dry, winters are cool and springs and autumns range from mild to balmy. The city also has the label of experien-

cing 'four seasons in one day'; the weather can be unpredictable at times, and it's best to be ready for a weather change at any time with an umbrella and extra layers of clothes. Spring and autumn generally have the most comfortable temperatures. In winter, the temperature drops to below 5°C (41°F) at night while in summer, extremely uncomfortable hot days over 40°C (104°F)

Below: the signs of bushfire can be seen in the Grampians; always adhere to local advice on lighting fires.

Essentials

A ustralia is a relatively safe country. That being said, you should exercise the same common sense and precautions as you would elsewhere regarding your possessions and personal security. Issues surrounding prostitution, drugs and drunken behaviour occur as in all cities, but these are unlikely to affect travellers. More likely to affect you are Australia's extremely strict regulations about what can and cannot be brought into the country. There are heavy fines for false or inaccurate claims. It is always best to declare an item if in doubt. Log on to www.customs.gov.au for more information.

EMBASSIES AND CONSULATES

British Consulate General
17th Floor, 90 Collins Street; tel: 03-9652 1600 (office hours) or 02-4422 2280 (after-hours emergencies); http://ukinaustralia.fco.gov.uk/en/

Irish Embassy
20 Arkana Street, Yarralumla, Canberra; tel: 02-6273 3022; www.embassyofireland.au.com

United States Consulate General
553 St Kilda Road; tel: 03-9526 5900; melbourne.usconsulate.gov

EMERGENCIES

For police, fire or ambulance dial: **000**.

The biggest health hazard in Australia is the sun, which has the potential to burn even on cloudy days. Wear SPF30+ sunblock at all times. Water safety is also an issue: swim only at beaches that are patrolled by lifesavers, and between the yellow and red flags. Never swim at night after a few drinks.

ENTRY REQUIREMENTS

Visitors must have a passport valid for the entire period of their stay, and a visa that must be obtained before leaving home (except for New Zealand citizens, who are issued with a visa on arrival). Information on visa requirements is available from www.immi.gov.au.

HEALTH

No vaccinations are required for entry to Australia. For medical attention after working hours go to the casualty department of a major hospital. Medicare, Australia's public health care system, allows travellers from the UK, Ireland, New Zealand and selected other countries to receive free or discounted medical treatment, limited to public hospitals and visits to the doctor; see www.medicareaustralia.gov.au.

HOSPITALS

The Alfred Hospital
Commercial Road, Prahran; tel: 03-9276 2000; www.alfred.org.au; map p.117 D4

Royal Melbourne Hospital
Grattan Street, Parkville; tel: 03-9342 7000; www.rmh.mh.org.au

St Vincent's Hospital
41 Victoria Parade, Fitzroy; tel: 03-9288 2211; www.svhm.org.au; map p.121 E1

PHARMACIES

Chemist shops are a great place to go for advice on minor ailments such as bites or stomach troubles.

INTERNET CAFÉS

Click N Drag Internet Lounge
137a Acland Street, St Kilda; tel: 03-9534 0859; Mon–Fri 9am–7pm, Sat 10am–7pm, Sun noon–5pm; map p.119 D4

N2c
Shop 100, 200–2 Bourke Street, City Centre; tel: 03-9639 3220; daily 24 hrs; map p.121 D2

MONEY

The local currency is the Australian dollar (A$), made up of 100 cents. Coins come in 5, 10, 20 and 50 cents units and 1 and 2 dol-

Left: a red-jacketed tourist information volunteer.

by the code of the country you are calling.

You can use your mobile's roaming capacity or buy a local SIM card kit and top it up with prepaid calls. Or get a phonecard to use the public phones. These are available from newsagents or outlets displaying the Telstra logo. Local calls from public phones cost 40 cents, regardless of time spent.

TIME ZONE
Melbourne time is 10 hours ahead of GMT, and 11 hours ahead during daylight savings.

TOURIST INFORMATION
Accredited Visitor Information Centres are marked with the blue and yellow 'i'. Red-jacketed volunteers can be found on the streets to help with enquiries.

Melbourne Visitor Information Centre
Federation Square; tel: 03-9658 9658; daily 9am–6pm; map p.121 D3

That's Melbourne
tel: 03-9658 9658
www.thatsmelbourne.com.au;

Visit Victoria
www.visitvictoria.com
www.visitmelbourne.com

lars. Notes come in 5, 10, 20, 50 and 100 dollar bills.

Banking hours are generally Mon–Thur 9am–4pm and Fri 9am–5pm. Some branches are open on Saturday mornings.

Carrying a credit or debit card is advised. ATMs are common throughout Melbourne; some charge a fee. Foreign-exchange bureaux are located at Melbourne Airport and throughout the city. The Travelex branch at 261 Bourke Street is open seven days a week. All major traveller's cheques can be cashed at banks.

POSTAL SERVICES
Australia Post offices are generally open between 9am–5pm Mon–Fri. Post offices in the CBD include one at 250 Elizabeth Street and another at 45 Collins Street. There are also postal agencies in some newsagents; www.auspost.com.au.

TAXES AND TIPPING
Tipping is not a custom in Australia and is not expected. You may choose

Above: police cars.

to tip at cafés or restaurants – 10 percent of the bill would be reasonable – and in taxis, you may round up the payment according to service received.

Australia also operates the Tourist Refund Scheme. Check www.customs.gov.au for more information.

TELEPHONES
The national code for Australia is 61 and the area code for Victoria is 03. If you are calling from overseas, drop the 0. For directory enquiries, dial 1223, and for international calls, dial 0011, followed

Fashion

Australians are generally renowned for their relaxed style, but in Melbourne you will notice that the locals raise the style stakes, with a lot more people dressing up and experimenting with their individual look. Most fashionistas saunter along Chapel Street, which is lined with great boutiques, in search of the latest looks, while bargain-hunters zero in on Smith Street for its factory outlets. The city also has hip independent designer markets where you can scour through the massive range of quirky, one-of-a-kind products you won't be able to find elsewhere. *See also Markets, p.72, and Shopping, p.96.*

AKIRA ISOGAWA
GPO, Level 1, 350 Bourke Street, City Centre; tel: 03-9663 5003; www.akira.com.au; Mon–Thur 10am–6pm, Fri 10am–8pm, Sat 10am–6pm, Sun 11am–5pm; tram: 96; map p.121 C2
This celebrated designer combines his Japanese heritage with a relaxed Australian style. To create a contemporary look, he fuses old and new by using kimono silks alongside modern fabrics.

ALANNAH HILL
Melbourne Central, 300 Lonsdale Street, tel: 03-9639 6399; www.alannahhill.com.au; Mon–Thur 10am–6pm, Fri 10am–9pm, Sat 10am–6pm, Sun 10am–5pm; train: Melbourne Central; map p.121 C2
For all things pretty and

Held in March every year, L'Oréal Melbourne Fashion Festival (www.lmff.com.au) is a premium consumer event that promotes the Australian fashion industry. The event showcases the autumn/winter collections when they are available in store.

Above: at Bettina Liano's catwalk show.

floral, this is the go-to label. The famous and at times controversial designer continues to appeal to fashionistas with whimsical styles.

ALICE EUPHEMIA
Shop 6, Cathedral Arcade, 37 Swanston Street; tel: 03-9650 4300; www.aliceeuphemia.com; Mon–Thur 10am–6pm, Fri 10am–7pm, Sat 10am–6pm, Sun noon–5pm; train: Flinders Street; map p.121 D3
Founded in 1997, this space stocks only Australian made and designed clothing and one-off handmade jewellery.

BETTINA LIANO
Melbourne Central, 300 Lonsdale Street; tel: 03-9663 4804; www.bettinaliano.com; Mon–Thur 10am–6pm, Fri 10am–8pm, Sat 10am–5pm, Sun noon–6pm; train: Melbourne Central; map p.121 C2
This designer's sexy jeans and jersey dresses are sought after by many women including celebrities like Portia Di Rossi and Naomi Campbell, and, most recently, Lady Gaga.

COLLETTE DINNIGAN
553 Chapel Street, South Yarra; tel: 03-9827 2111; www.collettedinnigan.com.au; Mon–Thur 10am–6pm, Fri 10am–7pm, Sat 10am–5pm, Sun 11am–5pm; tram: 78, 79; map p.117 E3
Most famous for her beautiful handmade lingerie, Collette Dinnigan also designs high-end fashion using vibrant fabrics with beading and embroidery details.

COUNTRY ROAD
Australia on Collins, 260 Collins Street, City Centre; tel: 03-9650 5288; www.countryroad.com.au; Mon–Thur 10am–6pm, Fri

Left: Melbourne's laneways harbour many funky boutiques.

Yarra; tel: 03-9826 4240; www.waynecooper.com.au; Mon–Thur 10am–6pm, Fri 10am–7pm, Sat 10am–5pm, Sun 11.30am–5.30pm; tram: 78, 79; map p.117 E4
Originally from the UK, Wayne Cooper is another star on Australia's fashion scene. Gorgeous evening-wear with a clever play on textures and colours is his signature style. Besides his wearable womenswear, his collections also include menswear, kidswear, shoes, bags and accessories.

10am–8pm, Sat 10am–6pm, Sun 11am–5pm, tram: 112 map p.121 D3
This well-loved Australian brand was established in 1974, and continues to appeal with its clean, sleek look, for both sexes.

IN.CUBE8R GALLERY

321 Smith Street, Fitzroy; tel: 03-8415 0321; www.incube8r.com.au; Tue 11am–5pm, Wed–Sat 11am–6pm, Sun noon–4pm; tram: 86; map p.115 E2
This is organised like an interactive long-term 'market' or bazaar that leases out space for designers and artists to display their pieces. The gallery is partitioned into glass cabinets and racks, making it easy for shoppers to browse around and find one-off handmade items by over 80 designers. Designer goods featured include Adrienne Barrington's hand-crafted jewellery and accessories as well as Nearly Roadkill's unique bags, belts and wallets cleverly made from scrap materials like vintage car upholstery.

SABA

Melbourne Central, 300 Lonsdale Street; tel: 03-9650 9797; www.saba.com.au; Mon–Thur 10am–6pm, Fri 10am–9pm, Sat 10am–6pm, Sun 10am–5pm; train: Melbourne Central; map p.121 C2
Established in Melbourne in 1965, the contemporary-chic Saba brand is renowned within the fashion world. Women's and men's clothing are crafted with stunning fabrics. Saba's jeans are a highlight too.

SCANLAN & THEODORE

285 Little Collins Street, City Centre; tel: 03-9650 6195; www.scanlanandtheodore.com; Mon–Thur 10am–6pm, Fri 10am–9pm, Sat 10am–5pm, Sun noon–5pm; tram: 112; map p.121 C2
Scanlan & Theodore's sophisticated label is dedicated to women's independent beauty. For 20 years, its signature look has been well crafted, simple, clean and modern.

WAYNE COOPER

450–460 Chapel Street, South

ZIMMERMAN

GPO, 350 Bourke Street, City Centre; tel: 03-9663 9349; www.zimmermannwear.com; Mon–Thur, 10am–6pm, Fri 10am–8pm, Sat 10am–6pm, Sun 11am–5pm; tram: 96; map p.121 C2
One of Australia's most successful labels, the designs are inspired by the beach, with splashes of eclectic colours and prints. Feminine details are juxtaposed with sharp tailoring for womenswear. The label also features swimwear and lingerie.

Below: a tempting window display at Alannah Hill.

Festivals and Events

A week rarely goes by in Melbourne without something being celebrated. Being the cultural capital of Australia and filled with sports fans, it's no surprise that a host of top arts and sporting events take place here. World-class events include the Australian Open, the Melbourne International Comedy Festival and the Melbourne International Film Festival. Equally exciting but on a smaller scale are the city's Chinese New Year celebrations and 'Carols by Candlelight' during the Christmas season.

SUMMER (DEC–FEB)
Boxing Day Test
26 Dec: Melbourne Cricket Ground; train: Jolimont or Richmond; map p.117 D1
This cricket match is a great tradition and the most anticipated cricket match of the year. There are also several activities that take place around the MCG.

Australian Open Tennis Championships
Jan: Melbourne Park; www.australianopen.com; train: Richmond, Jolimont or Flinders Street; map p.116 C1
Tennis stars hit Melbourne for the first Grand Slam of

Below: at the Australia Open.

Christmas in Melbourne is not complete without Carols by Candlelight. This iconic Melbourne event has been running since 1937 and attracts thousands of people. Held at the Sidney Myer Music Bowl just before Christmas, this televised event sees a host of singers, performers, dancers and musicians joined in song. Of course, there's a visit from Santa too. It's also a major fundraising event for Vision Australia. www.visionaustralia.org.au.

the year. Played at the peak of summer, the heat is usually an issue for the players.

Midsumma
Jan/Feb: St Kilda; www.midsumma.org.au; tram: 96, 112
Victoria's premier gay and lesbian arts and cultural festival since 1988. Includes the pride march, through St Kilda to the beach.

St Kilda Festival
Feb: St Kilda; www.stkildafestival.com.au; tram: 96, 112
St Kilda's foreshore comes to life with the cream of

Australia's musical talents. Also includes comedians, performers, extreme sports, dance and children's entertainment.

Chinese New Year
Feb: Chinatown; www.chinesenewyear.com.au; train: Melbourne Central; map p.121 D2
Chinatown comes alive with fireworks, lions and cultural performances.

AUTUMN (MAR–MAY)
Melbourne Food and Wine Festival
Mar: all over Melbourne; www.melbournefoodandwine.com.au
The best of Australian and international producers are highlighted at this internationally acclaimed celebration of food and wine.

Australian Formula One Grand Prix
Mar: Albert Park; www.grandprix.com.au; tram: 96; map p.116 B4
Albert Park roars with the excitement of track and off-track events, providing a beautiful backdrop to this exciting sport.

Left: taking part in the Moomba Festival.

world. Events include debates, readings, literary banquets and workshops.

SPRING (SEPT–NOV)
Royal Melbourne Show
Sept: Melbourne Showgrounds, Epsom Road, Ascot Vale; www.royalshow.com.au; tram: 57
The country comes to town for 11 days. Features animals and livestock, carnival rides, music and even fireworks. Great for families.

Melbourne Fringe Festival
Sept/Oct: various venues; www.melbournefringe.com.au
Melbourne shows off its alternative side, with comedy, music, cabaret, dance and visual arts events.

Melbourne International Arts Festival
Oct: various venues, www.melbournefestival.com.au
One of the major multi-arts festivals in the world, with world theatre, music, dance and opera.

Australian Motorcycle Grand Prix
Oct: Phillip Island; www.motogp.com.au; coach from Federation Square
Phillip Island provides a picturesque setting for this leg of the world championship. There are also off-track activities on offer.

Spring Racing Carnival
Nov: various venues; www.springracingcarnival.com.au
Australia's premier racing celebration, including the Melbourne Cup, 'the race that stops the nation'. With 50 days of world-class racing in a party atmosphere.

that showcases the cream of Australia's comedy crop.

Melbourne International Flower and Garden Show
Mar/Apr: Royal Exhibition Building and Carlton Gardens; www.melbflowershow.com.au; train: Parliament; map p.115 D2
The best of Australian gardening is displayed in the World Heritage-listed Royal Exhibition Building and surrounding Carlton Gardens.

WINTER (JUNE–AUG)
Melbourne International Film Festival
July/Aug: various cinemas and theatres; www.melbournefilmfestival.com.au
Unveiling the best of world cinema from over 50 countries, for 17 days. Also includes parties and special celebratory events.

Melbourne Writers' Festival
Aug/Sept: Federation Square; www.mwf.com.au; train: Flinders Street; map p.121 D3
Attracting more than 400 writers from around the

Above: demonstrations at the Flower and Garden Show.

Moomba Festival
Mar: various city-wide venues; www.moombafestival.com.au
Held on the Labour Day long weekend (second Monday in March), Moomba is a massive outdoor festival held along the waterfront, in city streets and parks.

Melbourne International Comedy Festival
Mar/Apr: all over Melbourne; www.comedyfestival.com.au
One of the world's biggest and best comedy festivals

49

Film

There is a thriving independent cinema scene in Melbourne, and the number of independent filmmakers has been growing over the years. To get a feel of some of their work, check out www.innersense.com.au/mif/. Mainstream cinema has made its mark in this city too, with an increasing number of Hollywood movies being shot in Melbourne. It comes as no surprise, then, to find out that the city has also produced a number of actors who have found success in Hollywood and international fame – some of whom have even won an Oscar.

MELBOURNE FILM ICONS

Australia has produced, in recent years especially, a host of actors who have made it big in Hollywood. These include Nicole Kidman, Russell Crowe and Hugh Jackman.

Melbourne has not been left behind in this revolution either, being responsible for big names such as Eric Bana and Cate Blanchett. Bana's Hollywood credits include *Black Hawk Down* (2001), *Hulk* (2003), *Troy* (2004), *Munich* (2005), *Star*

Below: the Melburnian star Cate Blanchett.

Trek (2009) and *The Time Traveller's Wife* (2009). Blanchett won an Oscar for Best Performance by an Actress in a Supporting Role in 2005 for her appearance in *The Aviator* (2004). She has also acted, to great acclaim, in movies such as *Notes on a Scandal* (2006), *I'm Not There* (2007), *Elizabeth* (1998) and its sequel, *The Golden Age* (2007) and *The Curious Case of Benjamin Button* (2008). Other notable actors who hail from Melbourne include Rachel Griffiths *(Muriel's Wedding, Hilary and Jackie*, TV's *Brothers and Sisters)*, Radha Mitchell *(Pitch Black, Phone Booth, Melinda and Melinda)*, as well as up-and-coming actors, brothers Chris *(Star Trek)* and Liam *(The Last Song)* Hemsworth.

FILMS SHOT IN MELBOURNE

On The Beach (1957) was one of the earliest Hollywood movies filmed in Melbourne, starring icons Gregory Peck, Ava Gard-

ner and Fred Astaire. *Mad Max* (1979) – starring the then unknown Aussie actor Mel Gibson – was also shot in Melbourne.

In the 21st century, Hollywood has again come calling, filming movies such as *Charlotte's Web* (2006), *Ghost Rider* (2007), *Knowing* (2009) and *Where the Wild Things Are* (2009) in the city. It has also provided the backdrop for the TV series *The Pacific* (2010), produced by Steven Spielberg and Tom Hanks. For more information on films shot in this city, log on to www.filmedin melbourne.com.au.

CINEMAS

Melbourne has a strong arthouse cinema scene, while mainstream multiplexes are located across the city and suburbs.

Tuesdays are generally cheap movie days, when tickets are available at a lower price. However, some cinemas observe this tradition on other days, so check websites for details.

Left: catch a film atop the Rooftop Cinema.

The high-profile Melbourne International Film Festival (www. melbournefilmfestival.com. au) is held in July/August each year at venues across central Melbourne. Over 17 days, the world's best as well as emerging talents are showcased here. An iconic Melbourne event, there are a range of special events held around it. The festival is one of the oldest in the world, celebrating 60 years in 2011.

Left: Nicolas Cage in Melbourne-shot *Knowing*.

Cinema Nova
380 Lygon Street, Carlton; tel: 03-9349 5201; www. cinemanova.com.au; tram: 1, 8; map p.115 D2
Melbourne's largest art-house cinema complex.

Hoyts Melbourne Central
Melbourne Central Shopping Centre, City Centre; tel: 1300 357 357; www.hoyts.com.au; train: Melbourne Central; map p.121 C2
With cineplexes all over Melbourne, this is Hoyts' most central venue.

IMAX Melbourne Museum
Melbourne Museum Precinct, Rathdowne Street, Carlton Gardens, Carlton South; tel: 03-9663 5454; www.imaxmel bourne.com.au; daily from 9.45am; train: Parliament; tram: 86, 96, or free City Circle Tram; map p.115 D3
Documentaries, 3D films and often the latest mainstream films are featured on the massive IMAX format.

CINEMAS
ACMI (Australian Centre for the Moving Image)
Federation Square, Melbourne; tel: 03-8663 2200; www.acmi. net.au; daily 10am–6pm; train: Flinders Street; tram: free City Circle Tram; map p.121 D3
Featuring rare, arthouse and cult films.

Astor Theatre
Corner of Chapel Street and Dandenong Road, St Kilda; tel: 03-9510 1414; www.astor-theatre.com; Sun from 1pm, Mon–Sat from 6.30pm; train: Windsor; map p.119 E2
Art Deco-style space featuring cinema classics and some latest releases.

Moonlight Cinema
Royal Botanic Gardens, Birdwood Avenue, South Yarra; tel: 1300 551 908; www.moonlight. com.au; Dec–Mar, gates open 7pm; tram: 8; map p.116 C2
Screens latest releases, contemporary, cult and classic movies outdoors. Bring a picnic basket.

Rooftop Cinema
On top of Curtin House, 252 Swanston Street, City Centre; tel: 03-9663 3596; www. rooftopcinema.com.au; Dec–Apr, gates open 8pm; train: Melbourne Central; map p.121 C2
Relax in a deckchair and get distracted by the skyscrapers towering above.

Sun Theatre
8 Ballarat Street, Yarraville; tel: 03-9362 0999; www.sunthea tre.com.au; train: Yarraville
Six cinemas, all stunningly decked out in Art Deco style, dating back to 1938.

Village Cinemas Crown
Shop 50, 8 Whiteman Street, Southbank; tel: 1300 555 400; www.villagecinemas.com. au; train: Flinders Street; map p.120 C4
There are 13 cinemas at the Crown Entertainment Complex.

Food and Drink

Restaurants in Melbourne function as global culinary incubators; many locally trained young chefs leave for further experience abroad, where they end up forging stellar reputations. The favour is returned by scores of talented overseas chefs who are lured here by peerless fresh produce, exciting fusions of flavours, a devoted foodie culture and an attitude to fine dining without the flashiness. Of course there is a plethora of international cuisine to be had, from Asian to African and Middle Eastern. It's not possible to stay hungry in this city, which has a deserved foodie reputation internationally.

MELBOURNE'S CUISINE

There's no one tag for Melbourne's cuisine. You can eat everything from classic French dishes to spicy Malaysian hawker food, simple Mediterranean favourites to molecular gastronomy. The only thing that's uniform is the excellence and affordability of the local food and wine – indulging your tastebuds here is a supremely satisfying experience.

FRESH PRODUCE

Fresh, locally sourced produce is used by chefs across the city, with many having a particular penchant for organic artisan ingredients. Menus are

Melbourne has scores of excellent reasonably priced eateries, including those that are tucked away in narrow laneways or arcades. *Cheap Eats*, published by *The Age*, is filled with insider's tips on these places and feature as many as 58 cuisines for you to choose.

likely to specify meat producers (grass-fed and Wagyu beef from East Gippsland is favoured), the provenance of cheese (look out for offerings from Gippsland and the Yarra Valley), where salt is sourced (the pink grains from Murray River are often used) and the waters from which seafood has been

plucked (Pacific oysters and Coffin Bay scallops from South Australia are hugely popular).

INTERNATIONAL INGREDIENTS

Imported artisan products also feature, with tapas bars using Ortiz anchovies, jamón serrano and queso manchego, and Italian restaurants eschewing local equivalents for the best Carnaroli and Vialone Nano rice, Parmigiano Reggiano cheese and Italian olive oils (although the quality of local olive oil is improving every day).

INTERNATIONAL CUISINE

Italian, French and Cantonese cuisines have long pedigrees in Melbourne, but food from Spain, Lebanon, Morocco, Thailand, Malaysia, Turkey, Vietnam and Ethiopia is becoming increasingly popular, and many of the city's most exciting restaurants showcase these cuisines.

Interestingly – and perhaps this is the key to

Below: creative presentation of tasty local seafood.

Left: find great-value cafés in Melbourne's laneways.

There are only two restaurants in town with three-hat status: **Jacques Reymond** in Windsor and **Vue de Monde** in central Melbourne. Both offer simply extraordinary dining experiences. These places are expensive – set menus hover around A$150 per person – and have wonderful wine lists. You will need to book ahead for both, and Vue de Monde insists on receiving credit-card details when reserving a table; if you don't show, you will be charged for the meal regardless.

Other notable high-end restaurants include **Nobu** and **Rockpool Bar & Grill** at Crown Casino. St Kilda has **Circa** at the Prince hotel, South Yarra has **The Botanical** and Central Melbourne has **Taxi Dining Room** and **ezard** at The Adelphi hotel. You should dress to impress at all of these, and also come with a fully charged credit card.
SEE ALSO RESTAURANTS, P.88

MID-RANGE RESTAURANTS

This is the category that Melburnians love the most. Often, the food on

the success of Australian cuisine generally – a chef will draw on cuisines from across the globe for inspiration and when putting together a menu. A fragrant red Thai curry might sit next to a perfectly chargrilled rib-eye served with mash, and a delicate panna cotta might share the spotlight with mango-topped sticky rice. In Melbourne the brave new world of contemporary international food is as exciting as it is assured.

WHERE TO EAT

Some cuisines are strongly associated with particular streets or suburbs. For instance, Lygon Street is lined with Italian eateries, and Footscray, Richmond and Springvale are known for their authentic Vietnamese restaurants. Most suburbs have eating options in every budget category, although restaurants at the higher end of the spectrum tend to be found in central

Melbourne, Southbank, South Yarra and St Kilda.

HIGH-END RESTAURANTS

Australians are an egalitarian bunch and tend to view formal fine-dining establishments with a certain degree of suspicion. Epicures are just as likely to get excited about the menu at an edgy inner-suburban tapas bar as they are at restaurants in possession of a rare three-hat rating (see box, p.54), and those who dine out regularly tend to focus their attention on one- or two-hat establishments.

Right: a busy kitchen at a city centre restaurant.

offer is just as impressive as that served in the high-end establishments, the differences being that the vibe will be more casual, the wine lists less encyclopaedic, the service less formal and the prices more reasonable. The vast majority offer menus heavy on Mediterranean choices, with occasional forays into Asia.

Many of these places match a stylish interior with an impressive menu, interesting wine list and professional service. Two-hat places sitting comfortably in this category include **Grossi Florentino**'s upstairs restaurant, **Donovans**, **Stokehouse**, **Café Di Stasio** and **Cutler & Co.** in Fitzroy, which was also named best new restaurant by *The Age Good Food Guide 2010 (see box, right)*.

SEE ALSO RESTAURANTS, P.89

ETHNIC RESTAURANTS

In times past, describing a Melbourne restaurant as 'ethnic' hinted at over-spiced dishes (usually with Indian overtones), a hippie interior and Ravi Shankar

on the sound system. Not any more, though. After a week or so here, visitors to Melbourne inevitably opine that the most exciting and enjoyable restaurants are those that combine a designer interior with a bustling ambience and specific ethnic cuisine. Supreme among these are the Spanish **MoVida**, pan-Asian **Gingerboy**, Thai **Longrain**, Lebanese/Persian **Rumi** and Turkish **Gigibaba**.

Yum cha (dim sum) is a weekend pastime for many, as is a pre-dinner tapas indulgence or an antipasti-fuelled aperitivo in an inner-city bar-cum-restaurant.

Also of note is the takeaway food on offer here. Streets such as Sydney Road in Brunswick are littered with places specialising in cheap and tasty falafel sandwiches and *pides* (Turkish pizza-like flatbread), and you will find rice-paper rolls and *pho* (noodle soup) in many Footscray and Richmond cafés. Whether you are after a samosa, souvlaki or sushi roll, you

are bound to find a vendor somewhere.

SEE ALSO RESTAURANTS, P.89

PUBS

The phenomenon of the gastropub hasn't really hit Melbourne. Instead, many corner pubs across the inner city have been reinvented as attitude-free drinking zones that have undergone funky fit-outs and offer well-priced and imaginative bar meals. Notable examples include the **Lincoln Hotel** in Carlton and the **Builders Arms** in Fitzroy, but there are many others where the menu is more likely to feature a spicy calamari stir-fry or fragrant chicken tagine than it is a plate of steak, eggs and chips. Those pubs with a beer garden tend to be hugely popular in summer.

SEE ALSO BARS AND PUBS, P.34

DRINKS

BEER

Most Aussies like a beer or two. Brits might get a shock when they realise that lager, rather than ale, is all that's on offer, but they are usually swiftly reconciled to their fate. You will find the local drops Carlton and VB on tap at

Left: eating out is one of the top Melburnian pastimes.

Right: pubs are popular for meals as well as drinking.

most pubs, and bars tend to have one of the two on tap as well. Boutique alternatives such as Cooper's, Cascade, Mountain Goat and Little Creatures are often available on tap and always in bottles. Imported beers are also widely available. There are three glass sizes: a glass (200ml), pot (285ml) or pint (570ml).

WINE

Australia is one of the most highly respected New World wine-producing countries. Regions such as the Barossa, Coonawarra, Clare Valley, Margaret River, Yarra Valley and Mornington Peninsula produce exceptionally fine vintages year after year, and locals are just as likely to order a glass of shiraz or sauvignon blanc when they go out for a drink or beer. Those keen to sample Victorian wines should opt for Shiraz from the Heathcote region, Pinot Noir, Chardonnay or sparkling wine from the Yarra Valley, or Pinot Noir and Chardonnay from the Mornington Peninsula, Bellarine Peninsula and Gippsland. James Halliday's *Australian Wine Companion* website (www.winecompanion.com.au) and *Wine Atlas of Australia* are excellent references for those wanting to learn more about local wines.
SEE ALSO VINEYARDS, P.108

WHERE TO BUY FOOD
Ceres Organic Market
Corner of Roberts and Stewart Streets, Brunswick East; tel: 03-9389 0100; www.ceres.org.au; Wed and Sat 9am–1pm; tram: 112

This food and craft market featuring organic produce is held every Wednesday and Saturday morning. Local artisans sell a range of items, including handmade clothing, natural skincare products and recycled goods. There are also local organic sourdough breads and pastries, fairtrade coffees, teas and Australian chocolates, as well as biodynamic wines and organic spirits.

David Jones Foodhall
310 Bourke Street (Bourke Street Mall); tel: 03-9643 2222; www.davidjones.com.au; Mon–Wed 9.30am–7pm, Thur–Fri 9.30am–9pm, Sat 9am–7pm, Sun 10am–7pm; tram: 96; map p.121 C2
A gourmet wonderland offering delicacies from Australia and around the world as well as fresh produce. Within the basement are a delicatessen, cheese counter, patisserie and liquor store. It's an ideal pit-stop in during your shopping spree.

Haighs Chocolates
Shop 7–8, The Block Arcade, 282 Collins Street, City Centre; tel: 03-9654 7673; www.haighs chocolates.com.au; tram: 112; map p.121 C3
This is Australia's oldest family-owned chocolate-manufacturing retailer, established since 1915. It makes chocolate from raw cocoa beans, and more than 50 percent of the products are handmade.

Simon Johnson
12–14 Saint David Street, Fitzroy; tel: 03-9644 3630; www.simonjohnson.com.au; Mon–Fri 10am–6pm, Sat 9am–5pm, Sun 10am–4pm; tram: 112; map p.115 E2
This is one of the best spots to head to for homegrown and imported gourmet foods. It specialises in different types of olives and olive oils, cheeses and artisanal food.

Below: Haighs Chocolates offers handmade goodies.

55

Gay and Lesbian

Melbourne has a thriving gay and lesbian scene. Clusters of the gay community exist around Commercial Road in Prahran, Smith Street in Collingwood, Brunswick Street in Fitzroy, High Street in Northcote and Sydney Road in Brunswick. Daylesford, a couple of hours' drive out of Melbourne, has one of the largest gay populations in regional Australia. *BnewS* and the *Melbourne Community Voice (MCV)* are free publications you can find in cafés and bars, while JOY (94.9 FM) is Melbourne's radio station for the gay, lesbian, bisexual, transgender and intersex community.

ORGANISATIONS
Alternative Lifestyle Organisation (ALSO) Foundation
Level 8, 225 Bourke Street; tel: 03-9660 3900; www.also.org.au; map p.121 D2
For information on events and organisations serving the gay community.

Gay and Lesbian Switchboard
Tel: 03-9663 2939; www.switchboard.org.au
Provides counselling and information services.

Gay and Lesbian Tourism Australia
www.galta.com.au
Promotes gay-owned or gay-friendly accommodation and tour operators via its website.

GAY-FRIENDLY VENUES
DT's Hotel
164 Church Street, Richmond; tel: 03-9428 5724; www.dtshotel.com.au; train: West Richmond
Cosy pub with drag shows, pool, regular barbecues and even a wine club.

Above: in the gay-only Laird Hotel bar.

Glasshouse Hotel
51 Gipps Street, Collingwood; tel: 03-9419 4748; www.glass-house.com.au; train: Collingwood
Open to both gays and lesbians; women-only nights are on every second and fourth Saturday.

Greyhound Hotel
1 Brighton Road, St Kilda; tel: 03-9534 4189; www.ghhotel.com.au; tram: 67, 3/3a; map p.119 E3
A relaxed pub featuring drag shows, karaoke and music.

Laird Hotel
149 Gipps Street, Abbotsford;

tel: 03-9417 2832; www.laird hotel.com; train: Collingwood
Australia's longest running men-only gay hotel, catering to the leather, bear and alternative crowd, open seven nights a week with boutique accommodation.

Market Hotel
143 Commercial Road, South Yarra; tel: 03-9826 0933; www.markethotel.com.au; train: Prahran; map p.117 E4
Gay nightclub with live performances and drag productions.

The Peel
Corner of Peel and Wellington Streets, Collingwood; tel: 03-9419 4762; www.thepeel.com.au; train: Collingwood
Sweaty dance club with retro night on Sundays.

Xchange Hotel
119 Commercial Road, South Yarra; tel: 03-9867 5144; www.xchange.com.au; train: Prahran; map p.117 E4
Popular venue with video dance arena and drag shows five nights a week.

Left: partying at the Glasshouse Hotel.

SAUNAS

55 Porter Street
55 Porter Street, Prahran; tel: 03-9529 5166; train: Prahran; map p.117 E4
This popular sauna has a huge spa, a solarium and dry and steam saunas.

Club80
8–10 Peel Street, Collingwood; tel: 03-9417 2182; www. club80.net; train: Collingwood
Originally founded in Sydney, this is a well-equipped cruise environment for gay and bisexual men. There's room for socialising, internet connection and even art house cinema viewing.

Subway Sauna
Vault 13 Banana Alley Vaults, corner of Flinders and Queensbridge Streets, City Centre; tel: 03-9620 7766; www.subway sauna.com.au; train: Flinders Street; map p.121 C4
Subway is located right in the heart of the CBD and is open daily, 24 hours a day.

Ten Plus
59 Porter Street, Prahran; tel: 03-9525 0469; www.tenplus. com.au; train: Prahran; map p.117 E4
Ten Plus has been around for 15 years, mostly targeting non-scene guys. There are three areas in two buildings for cruising.

Wet On Wellington
162 Wellington Street, Collingwood; tel: 03-9419 2010; www. wetonwellington.com.au; train: Collingwood
Melbourne's only sauna with a swimming pool; there's also a licensed bar, a rooftop sundeck and private rooms. Free internet.

Under-18s won't have to miss out on all the fun as they can check out **Minus18**, the largest hangout for gay teens in the city. Events organised include dance parties and pizza arvos. Plus there are links to resources and MinusTV with episodes and podcasts for gay youths that are not shown on conventional TV. www.minus18.org.au.

EVENTS

ChillOut
The largest gay and lesbian festival in regional Victoria is held at Daylesford (www. chilloutfestival.com.au). It's dedicated to celebrating gay, lesbian, bisexual, transgender and queer pride within the unique backdrop of rural Victoria.

Melbourne Queer Film Festival
The MQFF (www.mqff.com. au) showcases the best in Queer cinema. It also supports emerging Australian filmmakers with a jury award for the City of Melbourne Best Australian Short Queer Film.

Midsumma Festival
Melbourne's annual Queer Celebration (www.mid summa.org.au) attracts over 100,000 people and takes place over three weeks from mid-January. First started in 1988, the event is spread over six municipalities and located in over 70 venues across the city. It's Victoria's premier gay and lesbian arts and cultural festival and brings together a diverse mix of artists and performers. Look forward to theatre, visual art, cabaret, film, live music and sports, amongst others.

Below: a Midsumma reveller.

History

1802
The crew of the *Lady Nelson* are the first white men to enter the Port Phillip Bay area.

1834
Pastoralists (livestock farmers) from Van Diemen's Land establish Victoria's first long-term settlement at Portland on Bass Strait.

1835
Farmer John Batman makes a treaty with the Wurundjeri for 240,000 hectares (592,800 acres) of land in Port Phillip's shores, giving them blankets and trinkets in payment; Batman and businessman John Pascoe Fawkner then found a white settlement on the banks of the Yarra River.

1837
The settlement is named in honour of British prime minister Lord Melbourne; surveyor Robert Hoddle lays out central Melbourne's grid system; the first inner-city land sale.

1842
The municipality of Melbourne is created.

1845
The Princes Bridge is constructed, linking the north and south banks of the Yarra River.

1847
Queen Victoria declares Melbourne a city.

1851
Melbourne is separated from New South Wales; gold is discovered in central Victoria, triggering a gold rush.

1852
75,000 gold-seekers arrive in the colony.

1853
The University of Melbourne is established.

1854
A railway between Port Melbourne and the central city is opened; the State Library of Victoria is founded.

1855
The Melbourne Museum is founded.

1856
Stonemasons win the right to an eight-hour day.

1857
The train line between the central city and St Kilda begins operation.

1858
The first games of Aussie Rules football are played.

1861
The Melbourne Cup is held for the first time – won by the horse Archer.

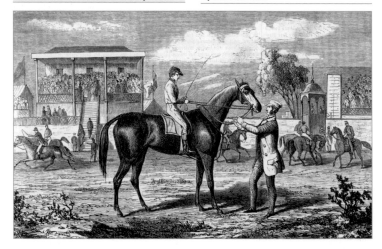

1877

The first Test cricket match is played at the MCG.

1880

Notorious bushranger Ned Kelly is captured in Glenrowan and hanged in Melbourne; the International Exhibition is held in the newly built Royal Exhibition Building.

1885

English journalist George Augustus Sala describes the city as 'Marvellous Melbourne'; the first cable-tram line opens.

1901

The federation of the six colonies becomes the Commonwealth of Australia; Melbourne is made the temporary parliamentary capital.

1906

The Melbourne Symphony Orchestra is formed.

1911

The city's most famous department store, the Myer Emporium, opens.

1927

Federal Parliament moves to the new national capital, Canberra.

1933

Melbourne's population passes the 1 million mark.

1942

Melbourne becomes the Allied headquarters for the Southwest Pacific in World War II.

1945

Australia embarks on an immigration programme; Melbourne attracts migrants from Greece, Italy and Malta.

1956

The Olympic Games are held in Melbourne.

1961

Melbourne's population passes 2 million.

1967

The first female city councillor is elected.

1973

The 'White Australia' policy is overturned and

Melbourne sees a huge increase in immigrants from Southeast Asia.

1902

City subway loop opens.

1990

Southbank Promenade is completed, opening the city to the southern banks of the Yarra.

1996

Development of the Docklands begins.

2002

Federation Square opens.

2006

Melbourne hosts the Commonwealth Games.

2008

Prime Minister Kevin Rudd officially apologises to Aboriginal Australians of the 'Stolen Generations'.

2009

Bushfires sweep through many parts of Victoria, including the Yarra Valley; deaths total nearly 200.

2010

Julia Gillard, whose private home is in Altona, a suburb in the western side of Melbourne, becomes Australia's first female prime minister.

Hotels

Melbourne offers a whole range of accommodation types, from luxury properties to boutique hotels and apartments. The best location in which to stay is the city centre, as it's easy to get from one place to another whether on foot or by tram. South Yarra has its luxury lodgings, while St Kilda is particularly beloved by backpackers. The inner north, including Carlton and Fitzroy, also tends towards budget and moderate accommodation options, and it's only a short tram or taxi ride to the city. Travellers who plan a trip to the surrounding regions in Victoria can stay overnight in a lush vineyard or by the sea.

THE CITY CENTRE

The Adelphi
187 Flinders Lane; tel: 03-8080 8888; www.adelphi.com.au; $$$$; train: Flinders Street; map p.121 D3
The brainchild of local architectural doyens Denton Corker Marshall (who designed the Melbourne Museum), The Adelphi is particularly notable for its whimsical, cantilevered rooftop lap pool. Recharge at the spa or dine at the famous **ezard** restaurant in the basement.
SEE ALSO RESTAURANTS, P.88

Alto Hotel on Bourke Street
636 Bourke Street; tel: 03-8608 5500; www.altohotel.com.au; $$$; train: Southern Cross, tram: 86, 95, 96; map p.120 B3

Price categories are for a standard double room including breakfast in the high season.
$ = under A$80
$$ = A$80–150
$$$ = A$150–220
$$$$ = over A$220

Above: the lap pool and sun deck at the Adelphi.

Alto Hotel markets itself as being environmentally friendly. Its emissions are offset, 'green-choice' electricity is used, and rainwater is utilised for cleaning. Rooms and apartments have a warm colour scheme and bathrooms have granite features; apartments have a kitchenette.

City Budget Hotel
22 Little Collins Street; tel: 03-9654 5401; www.citycentrebudgethotel.com.au; $$; train: Parliament; map p.121 E2
This family-run backpacker joint is in the midst of one of the most happening bar enclaves in the city. There's free WiFi, a roof terrace and laundry facilities. Rooms have a television, fridge, fans (no air conditioning) and tea- and coffee-making facilities; bathrooms are shared.

Grand Hyatt Melbourne
123 Collins Street; tel: 03-9657 1234; www.melbourne.grand.hyatt.com; $$$$; tram: 112; map p.121 D2
This hotel is nothing short of luxury. The ostentatious designs display an abundance of brass and marble right down to the

Left: the grand facade of the Hotel Windsor.

they are spacious. A sleek restaurant and bar is ideal to relax in after a day's exploration.

Hotel Windsor
111 Spring Street; tel: 03-9633 6000; www.thehotelwindsor. com.au; $$$$; train: Parliament; map p.121 E2
Located opposite Parliament House, this grande dame's rooms and public spaces are conservatively decorated. The traditional daily afternoon tea served in the lounge is a Melbourne institution.

InterContinental Melbourne The Rialto
495 Collins Street; tel: 03-8627 1400; www.ichotelsgroup.com; $$$$; tram: 112; map p.120 C3
Housed in an 1891 historic building, this luxury hotel boasts stunning, well-restored interiors. The suites are especially plush, and the indoor pool and spa offer the ultimate in relaxation. The location right in the middle of the CBD is a huge plus point.

Jasper Hall
489 Elizabeth Street; tel: 03-8327 7777; www.jasper hotel.com.au; $$$; tram: 19, 57, 59; map p.120 C1
Jasper sports a rich colour scheme and funky aesthetic, making its claim to the boutique tag credible if not compelling. The hotel's location next to popular Queen Victoria Market is vibrant during the day but quiet at night.

Medina Grand Melbourne
189 Queen Street; tel: 03-9934 0000; www.medina.com.au;

Last-minute accommodation is usually available, the only exception being when high-profile sporting festivals and events, such as the Australian Open (January), Australian Grand Prix (March), AFL Grand Final (September) and Spring Racing Carnival (November), are being held; at these times room rates rise and available rooms can be scarce, meaning that you should book well in advance. *See also Festivals and Events, p.48.*

huge black marble bathrooms. Its location makes it a popular site for business conventions, while its retail precinct lined with designer labels makes it a shopaholic's haven.

Hotel Causeway
275 Little Collins Street; tel: 03-9660 8888; www.hotel causeway.com.au; $$$–$$$$, train: 112; map p.121 C2
A stylish little number smack-bang in the centre of town, Hotel Causeway sports neat and nifty rooms. There's a gym and steam room, and a small

roof terrace. The rack rate is perhaps overpriced, but the weekend and summer specials are worth checking out.

Hotel Lindrum
26 Flinders Street; tel; 03-9668 1111; www.hotellindrum.com. au; $$$$; train: Flinders Street; map p.121 E2
Once a well-known billiard hall, Hotel Lindrum is now one of the city's best boutique hotels. It is conveniently located between the CBD and Yarra's sporting precinct. The rooms and suites are as stylish as

Below: Jasper Hall has a bright and bold colour scheme.

$$$; train: Melbourne Central, then taxi; map p.120 C3
The Medina chain operates a number of comfortable apartment hotels throughout Melbourne. This one has a great location, as well as a rooftop lap pool and a gym. The studio apartments are akin to a standard hotel room, while the rest have kitchen and laundry facilities with modern yet soothing decor.

Mercure Welcome Melbourne

265–281 Little Bourke Street; tel: 03-9639 0555; www.mercurewelcome.com.au; $$–$$$; tram: 96; map p.121 C2
No boutique or luxury credentials here, just clean, neat and well-equipped rooms in a central location. Major department stores are around the corner and the city's main tram route is directly in front of the hotel, making trips around Melbourne easy as pie. Check for online specials which can be half the rack rate.

Park Hyatt

1 Parliament Square, off Parliament Place; tel: 03-9224 1234; www.melbourne.park.hyatt.com; $$$$; train: Parliament; map p.121 E1
The central yet secluded location of this luxury pile opposite St Patrick's Cathedral almost seems at odds with its ostentatious decor, which was inspired by Las Vegas. All is forgiven, though, when the spacious rooms with king-sized beds and Italian marble baths are inspected. The hotel's facilities are among the best in town.

Punt Hill Little Bourke

11–17 Cohen Place; tel: 03-9916 8888; www.littlebourke.punthill.com.au; $$$; tram: 96; map p.121 D2
This attractive modern building in Melbourne's Chinatown offers comfortable apartments with kitchenettes and laundry facilities, while public facilities include a gym and an indoor lap pool. As befits the location, the building has been designed to meet feng shui requirements. Melbourne's major theatres are only a curtain call away.

Official Visitor Information Centres (identifiable by a yellow 'i' on a blue background) offer advice on all accommodation types and can often make bookings on your behalf. The classifieds and travel section of *The Age* newspaper on Saturdays can be a good source for new and offbeat places.

Robinsons in the City

405 Spencer Street; tel: 03-9329 2552; www.robinsonsinthecity.com.au; $$$$; train: Southern Cross; map p.120 A2
Housed in what was Melbourne's first commercial bakery, this 1850s building on the edge of the city centre offers an intimate accommodation experience. There is free WiFi and air conditioning in all rooms. Breakfast is prepared by the owner and served in the old bakehouse.

The Sebel Melbourne

394 Collins Street; tel: 03-9211 6600; www.mirvachotels.com/sebelmelbourne; $$$; train: 112; map p.120 C3
Spacious rooms and a prestigious Collins

Below: the pool at the Stamford Plaza, one of the hotel's many amenities.

Right: in the lobby of the Sofitel Melbourne on Collins.

Street address await at this popular apartment hotel. The apartments are equipped with ergonomic work desks, kitchenettes and laundry facilities, and there's an on-site gym for the athletically inclined.

Sofitel Melbourne on Collins
25 Collins Street; tel: 03-9653 0000; www.sofitelmelbourne.com.au; $$$$; train: 112; map p.121 C2

Located in the 'Paris End' of Collins Street, the Sofitel has rooms starting on level 36 of a high-rise tower. If your budget allows, opt for a luxury room or a suite, as the standard room is slightly cramped. There are bars and restaurants galore, a business centre and a fitness centre.

Stamford Plaza
111 Little Collins Street; tel: 03-9659 1000; www.stamford.com.au/spm; $$$–$$$$; train: Parliament; map p.121 D2

Located at the top end of town, the Stamford Plaza has amenities aplenty, including an indoor/outdoor pool, a restaurant, a bar and two gyms. All suites feature kitchenettes and bath-spas.

Vibe Savoy
630 Little Collins Street; tel: 03-9622 8888; www.vibehotels.com.au; $$$; train: Southern Cross; map p.120 B3

This intimate hotel within a 1920s heritage building promotes an elegant, club-like atmosphere. The fresh and hip vibe appeals to the modern generation, with the hotel in the midst of the bustle of the city. At the

end of the day, slink into the trendy Alexander Bar for a refreshing cocktail.

The Victoria Hotel
215 Little Collins Street; tel: 03-9669 0000; www.victoriahotel.com.au; $$; tram: 112; map p.121 D2

Those who like their accommodation to be smartly packaged should steer clear of the Victoria. Bargain-lovers will be thrilled, though, as prices are super-cheap. There's a rooftop gym, pool, sauna and spa, as well as an internet café, bar and restaurant.

Westin Melbourne
205 Collins Street; tel: 03-9635 2222; www.westin.com.au/melbourne; $$$$; train: Flinders Street, tram: 112; map p.121 D3

The Westin has an outstanding location overlooking St Paul's Cathedral and leafy Collins Street. Decor is stylishly understated, featuring muted colour schemes and excellent Australian contemporary art. Top marks go to the bar and restaurant spaces that allow you to relax indoors or on a terrace overlooking the City Square.

EAST MELBOURNE
Hilton on the Park Melbourne
192 Wellington Parade; tel: 03-9419 2000; www.melbourne.hilton.com; $$$$; tram: 75; map p.115 E4

This hotel on the eastern edge of the CBD offers luxury suites with views across Fitzroy Gardens. Sports fans will appreciate its proximity to the Melbourne Cricket Ground and Rod Laver Arena. Rooms are spacious yet warm, with large windows and WiFi access.

Knightsbridge Apartments
101 George Street; tel: 03-9470 9100; www.knightsbridgeapartments.com.au; $$–$$$; train: Jollimont; tram: 75; map p.115 E2

Close to the Fitzroy Gardens, Melbourne Cricket Ground and busy shopping and entertainment

Price categories are for a standard double room including breakfast in the high season.
$ = under A$80
$$ = A$80–150
$$$ = A$150–220
$$$$ = over A$220

Price categories are for a standard double room including breakfast in the high season.
$ = under A$80
$$ = A$80–150
$$$ = A$150–220
$$$$ = over A$220

precinct of Bridge Road in Richmond, these serviced studio apartments offer WiFi, an en-suite bathroom, a kitchenette with basic equipment and air conditioning. The decor is pleasant and rates are reasonable, particularly the last-minute deals.

CARLTON AND FITZROY
Downtowner on Lygon

66 Lygon Street; tel: 03-9663 5555; www.downtowner.com. au; $$$; tram: 1; map p.115 D3
The location here is perfect – halfway between the city centre and the bohemian enclave of Carlton. Rooms are attractive and well equipped, with king-sized beds and small en suites. Guests have free access to the Melbourne City Baths' pool and gym nearby. There's a restaurant and bar, but Lygon Street's alternatives are more alluring.

The Nunnery

116 Nicholson Street; tel: 03-9419 8637; www.nunnery. com.au; $–$$; tram: 96; map p.115 E2
This place offers three tiers of accommodation (a hostel, guesthouse and townhouse). Housed in three historic buildings including a former nunnery, its city-edge location faces the Carlton Gardens. Bathrooms are shared, there are fans and heaters in all rooms, and there's a communal kitchen and lounge in each building.

SOUTHBANK, DOCKLANDS, SOUTH WHARF AND SOUTH MELBOURNE
Crown Metropol

8 Whiteman Street, Southbank; tel: 03-9292 8888; www. Crownmetropol.com.au; $$$$; train: Flinders Street; map p.116 A2
This brand-new hotel is the ultra-trendy sister of the more lavish Crown Towers next door. The interior is adorned with original modern artwork by emerging and established artists. In the spacious rooms, Japanese 'shoji-inspired' sliding screens are used to divide the bathroom and bedroom. Slide them open if you want to create a sense of space, or shut them if you want privacy. Crown Metropol is also home to **Maze Melbourne** by Gordon Ramsay.
SEE ALSO RESTAURANTS, P.92

Crown Promenade Hotel

8 Whiteman Street, Yarra Bank; tel: 03-9292 6688; www. crownpromenadehotel.com. au; $$$$; train: Flinders Street;

Left: the Downtowner on Lygon is in an ideal location.

Most accommodation providers have their own websites. One of the easiest ways to book is online, where you can get cheap, last-minute deals through specialist 'clearing houses' for unsold rooms. If you are looking for the cheapest deal possible and willing to put in some effort, a worthwhile tactic can be to look up last-minute prices at these clearing houses, then contacting the hotel direct to see if it can undercut this, effectively saving you the commission. Try www.wotif.com or www.stayz.com.au.

map p.120 C4
Towering above the Yarra River, this hotel is next to the casino and entertainment complex that includes cinemas, restaurants and live entertainment. It is modern and stylish, with views over the river and Port Phillip Bay. Facilities include an indoor pool, steam rooms and two outdoor decks.

Docklands Apartments – Grand Mercure

23 St Mangos Lane; tel: 03-9641 7503; www.docklands servicedapartments.com.au; $$$$; train: Southern Cross, then taxi; map p.114 B4
This Grand Mercure setting is the largest serviced apartment complex by the waterfront in Melbourne. Next to the vibrant Waterfront City and close to the shopping district, it caters to both business and leisure travellers. The rooms are sleek and comfortable, matching its waterfront setting.

Hilton Melbourne South Wharf

2 Convention Centre Place, South Wharf; tel: 03-9027 2000;

Left: enjoy fantastic views from the Langham.

The suites feature elegant decor with plenty of luxurious touches. The in-house spa, posh restaurant and glam champagne bar ensure a sybaritic stay.

Manor House Apartments
36–38 Darling Street, South Yarra; tel: 03-9867 1266; www.manorhouse.com; $$$; train: South Yarra; map p.117 E3
Manor House has 40 apartments including double-storey and terrace suites. The well-furnished apartments are simple, clean and comfortable, with designer features and original local paintings. Facilities include a heated indoor pool, spa and gym.

ST KILDA
Base Backpackers Melbourne
17 Carlisle Street, St Kilda; tel: 03-8598 6200; www.stayat base.com/base-backpackers-melbourne-hostel; $; tram: 16, 96; map p.119 D3
This sleek operation markets itself as Australia's hippest hostel. Four- to eight-bed dorms have bunk beds, air conditioning, security lockers and private en suites; the 'Sanctuary Floor' is for females only.

www1.hilton.com; $$$$; train: Southern Cross, then taxi; map p.116 A2
The city's newest business precinct welcomes the opening of this incredibly stylish property just by the banks of Yarra River. It is the only hotel with direct access to the Melbourne Convention and Exhibition Center. Rooms either have views of the bay or the city.

Langham Melbourne
1 Southgate Avenue, Southbank; tel: 03-8696 8888; www.melbourne.langhamhotels.com.au; $$$$; train: Flinders Street; map p.121 D4
Southbank Promenade's trendy restaurants, Crown Casino and other attractions are just a few steps away from this elegant hotel. Step in and smell the aroma of ginger lily, a signature Langham scent, then luxuriate in one of the elegant rooms overlooking the Yarra River.

PRAHRAN, SOUTH YARRA, RICHMOND AND TOORAK
The Como Melbourne
630 Chapel Street, South Yarra;

tel: 03-9825 2222; www.mirvac-hotels.com/como-melbourne; $$$$; train: South Yarra; map p.117 E3
Many of the rich and famous wouldn't stay anywhere else. The Como offers suites with king-sized beds; some have a private Japanese garden and spa. Its location is close to the many temptations of Chapel Street and Toorak Road.

The Lyall
14 Murphy Street, South Yarra; tel: 03-9868 8222; www.thelyall.com; $$$$; train: South Yarra; map p.117 E3
This boutique hotel located on a leafy residential street off the upmarket South Yarra shopping and eating strip has the feel and decor of a private club.

Right: Base Backpackers in St Kilda is a great budget option.

There are laundry facilities and an internet café, and St Kilda's lively café, bar and beach scene is right on the doorstep.

Olembia Guest House
96 Barkly Street, St Kilda; tel: 03-9537 1412; www.olembia. com.au; $; tram: 16, 96; map p.119 D3

Olembia is a cosy and friendly guesthouse with good facilities, parking and a pleasant lounge. There is a communal area with an open fireplace, comfy lounges and dining room, ideal for meeting and exchanging the day's experiences with other guests.

The Prince
2 Acland Street, St Kilda; tel: 03-9536 1111; www.theprince. com.au; $$$–$$$$; tram: 16, 96; map p.119 C3

The über-stylish Prince was designed by the edgy architectural firm Wood Marsh. Rooms feature de luxe linen and distinctive artworks; the suites have fabulous views of Port Phillip Bay. The hotel's Aurora Spa is probably the best one in Melbourne, and the same encomium applies to the in-house Circa Restaurant.

St Marine Boutique Hotel
42 Marine Parade, St Kilda; tel: 03-9534 1311; www.stmarine.

com.au; $$–$$$; tram: 16, 96; map p.119 D4

A renovated Edwardian home overlooking St Kilda beach, which is only a few steps away. Rooms are light and airy, befitting its beachy setting and allowing the ocean breeze through; the bathrooms have retained the building's old-world charm.

AROUND THE BAY
Cape Schanck Lighthouse
420 Cape Schanck Road, Cape Schanck; tel: 03-5988 6184; www.austpacinns.com.au; $$; hire a car

Enjoy a slice of history and check into one of the three-bedroom self-contained old lighthouse-keeper cottages. There are no pampering facilities here, only a gas heater, cosy beds and a spacious living and dining room. Visits to the historic lighthouse and walks along the beautiful cliffs will make your stay extra-special.

Right: sunset over the Crowne Plaza Torquay.

Oceanic Motel Apartments
231 Ocean Beach Road, Sorrento; tel: 03-5984 4166; www.oceanicgroup.com.au; $$$; hire a car

These stylish private two-storey units are semi-self-contained, with microwave, fridge, dishwasher, crockery and TV. There is a living room that opens out to a private courtyard. Just a short stroll from the beach, lively cafés, boutiques and galleries in Sorrento.

YARRA VALLEY AND DANDENONG RANGES
Balgownie Estate Vineyard Resort & Spa
Corner of Melba Highway and Gulf Road, Yarra Glen; 03-9730 0700; www.balgownieestate. com.au; $$$$; hire a car

This resort and spa has elegant spa suites with views of the landscaped gardens and rolling vineyards. After wining and dining, make a booking at the Natskin Spa Retreat to de-stress for a few hours.

Healesville Sanctuary Park Cottages
85 Badger Avenue; tel: 03-5962 2904; www.sanctuarypark. com.au; $$$; hire a car

Only an hour's drive from Melbourne, Sanctuary Park is the perfect country escape. The private cottage accommodations offer amazing views of the surrounding mountains, wineries and vast landscape.

Olinda Como Cottages
1465 Mount Dandenong Tourist Road; tel: 03-9751 2264; www.

Left: the Prince in St Kilda is highly recommended.

comocottages.com; $$$-$$$$; hire a car

Ideal for quick weekend getaways, Como offers rustic, self-contained cottages in a lush setting. It caters to couples and groups; guests can request in-room massages, go for romantic walks in the gardens or just enjoy the warmth of a crackling open fire.

GREAT OCEAN ROAD
Apollo Bay

Seaview Motel and Apartments, 6 Thomson Street; tel: 03-5237 6660; www.seaviewmotel.com. au; $$; hire a car

A family-run business, Seaview is located along the Great Ocean Road and Otway Ranges, within easy reach of the sea. The rooms are clean and modern with free WiFi, and there is also a common barbecue area.

Crowne Plaza Torquay

100 The Esplanade; tel: 03-5261 1500; www.ichotels group.com; $$$$; hire a car

Modern design envelopes this huge new surf coast hotel, with every amenity catered for, and then some. After a game of tennis in the private courts or a workout in the gym, the spa is the ideal place to relax in with a pampering massage. The beachfront views are incomparable.

Cumberland Lorne

150 Mountjoy Parade; tel: 03-5289 4444; www.cumber land.com.au; $$$; hire a car

The Cumberland offers suites with wonderful views and complimentary recreational activities, right in the heart of this friendly town. The contemporary open-plan living in each apartment gives ample of space to unwind; with full kitchen and laundry amenities and a corner spa bath.

Hotel Warrnambool

Corner of Koroit and Kepler Streets, Warrnambool; tel: 03-5562 2377; www.hotel warrnambool.com.au; $$; hire a car

This contemporary boutique accommodation offers eight rooms with en-suite bathroom and four with shared bathroom. Families can choose interconnecting rooms if necessary. Other facilities include a shared kitchenette and laundry. After a day of sightseeing or whale-watching, unwind at the cosy bar or heated alfresco beer garden.

Below: unwind at the Cumberland Lorne.

Laneways

One of Melbourne's signatures is its labyrinth of laneways. Located in the city centre, this is where graffiti artists work, alternative bars flourish and bohemian boutiques proliferate. These laneways – such as Flinders Lane, Little Collins Street, Little Bourke Street and Little Lonsdale Street – are among the most vibrant thoroughfares in the CBD. Even the state's tourism campaign has highlighted the laneways urging visitors to 'Lose Yourself in Melbourne'. Indeed, the laneways are easy to get lost in at times, but they certainly are hidden gems, to both tourists and locals.

HISTORY

In 1837, Governor Richard Bourke's instruction to Melbourne's original surveyor Robert Hoddle was that he include laneways and alleyways within the grid pattern of the town plans. This was so that the various buildings could be serviced, through these little streets. The lanes then became home to hotels, stables and coach houses, gunsmiths, locksmiths, bakers, workshops and warehouses. Some even hosted brothels and other forms of illegitimate business. Many lanes have been renamed over time – some even in recent years – but what has remained is the fact that they are edgy streets waiting to be discovered.

PUBLIC ART

Not only are Melbourne's laneways a symbol of the city, they have also, increasingly, become the art of the city. Street art is vibrant and common, and certainly more so in

Above: street art is seen throughout the laneways.

its laneways. To carry on this proud history, the city began its Laneway Commissions programme in 2001. The annual commission seeks out concepts from artists for a series of contemporary public works. This can be in the form of an artwork, a project or an event. Most commonly, public art in Melbourne's laneways is seen in the form of both large and small spray-painted works, lightboxes, stencilling and papering.

SHOPPING

Retail therapy in Melbourne's laneways involves some quirky and exotic choices. You will get Melbourne – or Australian – fashion, souvenirs and some other surprises along the way too.

FOOD AND DRINK

For foodies who love to discover new things, Melbourne's laneways provide a host of cafés and restaurants filled with character. And if you fancy a drink, there's no shortage of bars either, especially at Hardware Lane. Centre Place (centreplaceonline.com) is a lively enclave housing vari-

> Many Chinese flocked to Melbourne during the gold rush of the 1850s, and some set up shops along Little Bourke Street. They eventually expanded into what is Chinatown today. This area is certainly worth a wander, especially Tattersalls Lane, Celestial Lane and Market Lane, which house popular Asian eateries.

Left: Melbourne's laneways are full of character.

The Mitre Tavern

5 Bank Place, Melbourne; tel: 03-9670 5644; www.mitretav ern.com.au; Mon–Fri 11am until late; map p.120 C3
Melbourne's oldest running pub, established in 1867, is still as popular as ever with office workers in the area. Syracuse, a well-known restaurant, is located in this small alley too.

MELBOURNE'S BEST LANES FOR ART
Cocker Alley

This lane contains a piece of work from world-famous street artist Banksy. It's a small stencil of a trench-coat-wearing figure in a scuba mask and is named *Little Diver*. It has been protected by a clear Perspex screen, to prevent vandalism.

Hosier Lane

One of Melbourne's most obvious attractions, this street screams cool. Marvel at the various forms of street art found here, as cartoons, ninjas, vampire faces and laughing skulls stare back at you. This lane also links to Rutledge Lane, where you'll find the Until Never gallery, which regularly displays work from emerging Australian underground artists.

Union Lane

The street art here is colourful, playful and powerful. The murals were first produced as part of the city's Graffiti Mentoring Project, where both professional artists and young volunteers produced the works.

ous coffee establishments, cafés and restaurants. Degraves Street is also a hive of activity particularly during lunch time.

Breadwell

135 Flinders Lane; tel: 03-9650 8544; Mon–Fri 7am–5pm; map p.121 D2
This quaint café is filled with old-fashioned comfort, and the vintage crockery is interesting too. A good place for cheap eats.
SEE ALSO CAFÉS, P.36

Degraves Espresso Bar

23–25 Degraves Street; tel: 03-9654 1245; Mon–Wed 7am–9.30pm, Thur 7am–10pm, Fri 7am–10.30pm, Sat 8am–6.30pm, Sun 8am–5.30pm; map p.121 D3
A groovy espresso bar that has a Parisian edge as well as an Art Deco interior. Drop by for coffee and conversation or tuck into a meal.

Max Bar & Restaurant

54–58 Hardware Lane; tel: 03-9600 1697; www.maxbar restaurant.com.au; Mon–Fri 11am–11pm, Sat–Sun 3pm–11pm; map p.120 C2
The oldest restaurant on the lane. Offers an impressive menu, with half-price cocktails Monday to Thursday.

Meyers Place Bar

20 Meyers Place; tel: 03-9650 8609; Mon–Thur 4pm –2am, Fri–Sat 4pm–4am; map p.121 D2
This is where the hip and trendy hang out. It's intimate, it's cosy and it's a guaranteed good night out.
SEE ALSO BARS AND PUBS, P.33

Below: the city's oldest pub is tucked down Bank Place.

Literature

In 2008, Melbourne was named by UNESCO as a City of Literature, only the second city to be awarded this honour, after Edinburgh in Scotland. Since then, two other cities have joined this list – Iowa City in the USA and Dublin in Ireland. The city boasts the largest literary publishing sector in Australia, and has more bookshops and readers than anywhere else in the country. It also hosts a wide range of literary festivals, such as the Melbourne Writers Festival, the Overload Poetry Festival and the Emerging Writers Festival. Local readers are also spoilt for choice by the great range of bookshops.

Above: the award-winning author Peter Carey.

AUTHORS AND POETS

Two of Australia's foremost 19th-century novelists, Rolf Boldrewood (Thomas Browne) and Marcus Clarke, lived in Melbourne. C.J. Dennis was the most famous of the city's early poets. His work *Songs of a Sentimental Bloke* (1916) told of daily life in the city.

In recent years, novelist Peter Carey has gained international popularity, with *The True History of the Kelly Gang* (2000) and *My Life as a Fake* (2003). He's one of only two writers who has been awarded the Man Booker Prize twice.

Indigenous writer Alexis Wright's *Carpentaria* (2006) won the 2007 Miles Franklin Literary Award, creating a milestone in the country's literary scene. Tony Birch is another indigenous writer whose poetry, short stories and novels have received critical acclaim.

Melbourne is also one of the world's leading cities for children's literature. Acclaimed writers include Wendy Orr (*Nim's Island*, 2000), Graeme Base (*Animalia*, 1986) and Andy Griffiths (*The Day My Bum Went Psycho*, 2001).

FURTHER READING
History
The Encyclopedia of Melbourne Edited by Andrew Brown-May and Shurlee Swain. This astonishing doorstep of a book runs from Abattoirs to Zoo and captures every facet of the city in between.

The Melbourne Book: A History of Now by Maree Coote. This book packs together interesting snippets of people, places and events that make the city.

Memoirs
Down Under by Bill Bryson. Covers Australia as a whole, including Melbourne and Victoria. The urbane, breezy style is deceptive; some serious research has gone into this entertaining travelogue.

My Life As Me by Barry Humphreys. Hilarious, highly polished reminiscence of growing up in 1950s Melbourne, the genesis of his various characters and the path to a level of worldwide acclaim that saw Dame Edna Everage (but not Humphreys) given the keys to her home city.

Unpolished Gem by Alice Pung. Leaving the

The American bookstore chain has an outlet right in the heart of the city centre, for all your literary needs.

Collins Booksellers
86 Bourke Street, City Centre; tel: 03-9662 9472; www.collinsbooks.com.au; Mon–Thur 9am–6.30pm, Fri 9am–8pm, Sat 10am–6pm, Sun 11am–5pm; map p.121 D2
This store has been around since the 1920s, which is reason enough to visit it. Most suburban outlets of Collins Booksellers also host ABC Centres, with books and DVDs from the TV station's ABC Shop.

Dymocks
Lower Ground Floor, 234 Collins Street, City Centre; tel: 03-9663 0900; www.dymocks.com.au; Mon–Wed 9am–6.30pm, Thur 9am–7pm, Fri 9am–9pm, Sat–Sun 10am–6pm; map p.121 D3
The oldest Australian-owned bookstore, Dymocks is a leading bookseller in the Asia-Pacific region.

Below: food-lovers should head to Books for Cooks.

Melbourne Writers Festival is the city's premier literary festival, where more then 400 writers from all over the world converge. Activities include readings, performances, debates and film screenings, to name just a few. It usually takes place in late Aug/early Sept; www.mwf.com.au.

Cambodia of Pol Pot as a child, Pung's assimilation to life in Footscray along with her extended family is the core of this revealing memoir.

Fiction
The Getting of Wisdom by Henry Handel Richardson. One of the classics of Australian literature, this coming-of-age novel, set in late 19th-century Victoria, plucks sizeable auto-biographical chunks from the life of Ethel Lindesay (the author behind the pseudonym).

My Brother Jack by George Johnston. Strong enough to have inspired two television adapta-tions, this is a saga of two brothers living through 1920s and 30s depression-era Melbourne. Rich and complex.

BOOKSTORES
Angus & Robertson
379 Collins Street, City Centre; tel: 03-9620 0378; www.angusrobertson.com.au; Mon–Fri 9am–4pm; map p.121 C3
With more than 30 stores in Melbourne alone, this chain was once known as 'the biggest bookshop in the world'.

Books for Cooks
233–235 Gertrude Street, Fitzroy; tel: 03-8415 1415; www.booksforcooks.com.au; Mon–Sat 10am–6pm, Sun 11am–5pm; map p.115 E3
This store sells new and second-hand books on everything culinary-related.

Borders
211 La Trobe Street, Melbourne Central Shopping Centre, City Centre; tel: 03-9663 8909; www.borders.com.au; daily 10am–7pm, Thur–Fri until 9pm; map p.121 C2

Markets

Melbourne has a good variety of markets that sell everything from food and wine to arts and crafts. There are well-known venues such as Queen Victoria Market and South Melbourne Market that have been around since the 19th century and continue to draw visitors, and also lively outdoor markets at the fringe of the city. There are also specialised markets that give local designers a platform to showcase their one-of-a-kind pieces. Craftsmanship is of high quality and items are made locally. Away from the city, there are also farmers' markets that offer handmade or artisan produce.

ARTS CENTRE
SUNDAY MARKET

100 St Kilda Road; www.thearts centre.net.au/sundaymarket; Sun 10am–5pm; train: Flinders Street; map p.121 D4

Every Sunday more than 150 stalls of Victoria's finest arts and crafts congregate at the trendy Southbank area. Just a short walk from Flinders Street Station, you will see the market just along the Yarra River. Browse through the handmade ceramics, leather book covers, jewellery, and scarves, before refuelling your stomach with delicious Turkish bread or hot profitijes (Dutch pancakes) made on the spot.

ESPLANADE
MARKET ST KILDA

Upper Esplanade, St Kilda, between Cavell and Fitzroy Streets; www.stkildamarket. com; Sun 10am–5pm; tram: 16, 96; map p.119 C3

About 200 artisans gather along the Upper Esplanade of St Kilda to show-

Above: find local artisans' work at Esplanade Market St Kilda.

case their contemporary artworks every Sunday. Founded in 1970, its aim was an outlet for local artists to sell their handmade artworks to the public. It's a great place for a stroll and to soak in the sea breeze while chatting with the artists about their pieces. There are

accessories, decorative items, paintings and other items made of a variety of materials such as wood, glass, paper, recycled materials.

PRAHRAN MARKET

163 Commercial Road, South Yarra; tel: 8290 8220; www. prahranmarket.com.au; Tue

Left: fresh produce for sale at Prahran Market.

The Market Square is a great place to have a bite or coffee and watch your kids enjoy themselves at the playground. Activities for children are organised here too, such as the Australian Farmyard Friends (Tuesdays, Thursdays and Sundays), where kids can meet, feed and pat a range of farm animals.

QUEEN VICTORIA MARKET

Corner of Victoria and Elizabeth Streets; www.qvm. com.au; Tue, Thur 6am–2pm, Fri 6am–5pm, Sat 6am–3pm, Sun 9am–4pm (closed most public holidays); train: Flagstaff or Melbourne Central; tram: catch one heading north along Elizabeth and William Streets, and alight at either the Franklin or Victoria Street corners; map p.120 B1

Established in 1878, this is Melbourne's most iconic market. A huge section is dedicated to stalls selling fruit, vegetables, meat, poultry, seafood and delicious delicatessen products such as antipasti, dips, hams, cheeses, breads and olive oils. Food aside, there are stalls selling clothing, accessories, souvenirs, books and knick-knacks to boot. A permanent fixture here is a van selling freshly made doughnuts – there is usually a long queue so you can't miss it. The venue is most popular at weekends when the atmosphere is buzzing,

South Melbourne Market's fashion market is organised in spring and autumn (Thursday nights). Independent clothing designers unveil their new designs at this venue. Stalls sell locally designed and made goods – including vintage and collectable clothing, accessories and jewellery. Not into fashion? Browse through the original artworks, photography, homeware and children's clothing. There is a bar and microbrewery on site topped with live music from local performers.

dawn–5pm, Thur dawn–6pm, Fri dawn–6pm, Sat dawn–6pm, Sun 10am–3pm; train: Prahran; tram: 72, alight at stop no. 30 near Chapel Street; map p.117 E4

A highly popular market frequented by local residents and visitors. Alongside fruit and veg, meat and organic food, there is a café, bakery, delicatessen, wine and boutique beer store. There is also a cooking school with a state-of-the-art kitchen on the premises.

Left: shoppers at Queen Victoria Market.

73

topped with entertainment courtesy of buskers. Queen Street is converted into an outdoor café area with children's rides on Sundays.

REVOLVER DESIGNER MARKET

229 Chapel Street, Prahran; tel: 03-9521 5985; second Thur every month, 6pm–10pm; train: Prahran; map p.119 E1

This 'market' offers high-quality locally designed clothing, jewellery and others. It is set up by Revolver Upstairs, an entertainment hotspot comprising a live band room and bar. Many Melburnian designers have been featured here, including Poise & Joske (hand-painted jewellery and artworks), Lab 305 (wooden jewellery), Milky Tees (T-shirts), Hopeless Lingerie (handmade lingerie and accessories) and Victoria Mason (silver jewellery collection inspired by everyday household objects like spoons).

ROSE STREET ARTISTS' MARKET

60 Rose Street; tel: 03-9419 5529; www.rosestmarket.com. au; Sat–Sun 11am–5pm; tram: 96, 112

Located in a former junkyard in Fitzroy's backstreets, this is Melbourne's first dedicated art and design market. Set up in 2004, its objective was to be an outlet for emerging designers to sell their work. All the products are crafted by the 60 stallholders themselves, and as many things are handmade, no two items are the same. Best of all, they are of very high quality. You will find leather products stitched entirely by hand, unique paintings, fancy homeware, one-of-a-kind clothing and quirky accessories such as cufflinks and pendants made out of old Scrabble or Lego pieces. Take your time to chat with the friendly designers about their creations, before popping in the on-site gourmet café (Kanteen) for a cuppa.

SHIRT AND SKIRT MARKET

1 St Heliers Street, Abbotsford; 040-866 0646; www. shirtandskirtmarkets.com. au; third Sunday of the month 10am–4pm; train: Victoria Park, then bus: 200, 201, 205, 207 along Johnston Street, alight near Clarke Street and walk to Heliers Street

Located within the charming grounds of the Abbotsford Convent near the Collingwood Children's Farm is this unique market that provides

Below: Camberwell Sunday Market sells second-hand goods.

emerging and independent local designers with the opportunity to gain exposure. The market has an 'Australian-made and/or design' policy, and buyers are assured of a huge range of 'one-off' or 'limited edition' pieces. There are over 60 individual stalls that vary from month to month, showcasing an eclectic mix of clothing, jewellery, bags, accessories, and homeware. After shopping, have brunch or tea at the Convent Bakery café, which serves freshly baked breads and pastries.

SOUTH MELBOURNE MARKET

Corner of Cecil and Coventry Streets; tel: 03-9209 6295; www.southmelbournemarket. com.au; Wed, Sat, Sun 8am–4pm, Fri 8am–5pm, Cecil Street restaurants extended hours; light rail: 96, tram. 109, 112, map p.116 A3

This is the oldest market in Melbourne, having been around since 1867. There are various sections selling fruits and vegetables, seafood, flowers,

One person's trash can sometimes be another person's treasure. Camberwell Sunday Market (www.sundaymarket. com.au; tel: 1300-367 712), held every Sunday from 6.30am–12.30pm, is a popular place for Melburnians to find usable second-hand items. 'Treasure hunters' who like to suss out hand-me-downs, pots and pans, tea sets or collector items can head to this outdoor market located in a car park on the western side of Station Street, behind the Burke Road shopping strip.

Above: a shoe outlet at South Melbourne Market.

speciality foods and deli items. When you are done with shopping, head to Cecil Street's sidewalk, lined with stalls preparing food on the side. Grab a seat and feast on all manner of international food from paella, tapas and teppanyaki to kebabs, Turkish mezze and dim sum (look out for the famous 'dim sim', a special steamed meat dumpling that Aussies especially love).

YARRA VALLEY REGIONAL FOOD GROUP'S FARMERS' MARKET

38 Melba Highway, Yarra Glen; tel: 03-9739 0122; www.yarra valleyfood.com.au and www. yering.com; every third Sun of the month 9am–2pm; hire a car or taxi

Away from the city, one of the most popular farmers' markets is held in the barn of Yering Station, Victoria's first vineyard, established in 1838. Yarra Valley Regional Food Group's Farmers' Market, founded 10 years ago, grew from the original 41 members to over 80 local food and wine producers. Some of the favourites include Fruition Bakery's organic wood-fired sourdough breads, granola and dukkah, Jam Lady Jam's preserves, condiments, pickles, vinegars and terrines, and You Scream I Scream's locally made ice cream. There are also artisan chocolates and fudge, and mountains of seasonal fruits to sink your teeth into.

Museums and Galleries

Art and culture are dominant aspects of Melbourne, and there are a large number of museums and galleries. If you are exploring the city by foot, you will notice a lot of Melbourne's art is outdoors in the streetscape. One of the best ways to find out what's going on is to buy a copy of *Art Almanac*, a monthly booklet with listings of galleries and exhibitions. It costs A$3 and is available from galleries, some bookshops and newsagents. You can also find the listings online at www.art-almanac.com.au.

THE CITY CENTRE

ACMI (Australian Centre for the Moving Image)

Federation Square, corner of Russell and Flinders Streets; tel: 03-8663 2200; www.acmi. net.au; daily 10am–6pm (closed on Christmas Day); free except for some exhibitions; train: Flinders Street; map p.121 D3

The moving image in all its forms is celebrated here – film, television and digital culture. A range of exhibitions, films, festivals, workshops and live events are held to give diverse audiences unsurpassed ways to engage with the moving image.

ACMI's doors opened in 2002, and it is one of Victoria's major cultural, tourist and learning attractions. New production and exhibition spaces were launched in 2009, creating more stimulating ways in which audiences can engage with the moving image. This move also introduced the new, permanent exhibition, Screen Worlds: The Story of Film, Television and Digital Culture, an interactive

Above: tracing history at the Immigration Museum.

piece that shows how each form of the moving image has evolved as a creative medium.

Chinese Museum

22 Cohen Place; tel: 03-9662 2888; www.chinesemuseum. com.au; daily 10am–5pm (closed Good Friday, Christmas Day and New Year's Day);

charge; train: Melbourne Central; map p.121 D1

Located right in the heart of Chinatown, this museum has five floors that include the 200-year history of the Chinese in Australia told through artefacts. Learn about the rich history of this district and check out the Dragon Gallery, which

Left: explore Chinese-Australian culture.

adults, free for children; train: Flinders Street, tram: free City Circle; map p.120 C4

Stop by here to get the stories of the real people from all over the world who have migrated to Victoria. What you will find here are re-creations of the real-life stories of the journey to Australia, told with a rich mix of moving images, personal and community voices, memories and memorabilia. Find out why these journeys were made, what happened when the people arrived, and the impact all this had on the indigenous communities. A visit to this museum is not just interesting, it's thought-provoking, moving and emotional. Permanent exhibitions include Immigrant Stories and Timeline, Leaving Home, and Customs Gallery, which tells the story of the Old Customs House, where the museum is now housed.

Victoria Police Museum

World Trade Centre, Lower Concourse Level, 637 Flinders Street; tel: 03-9247 5214; www.police.vic.gov.au; Mon–Fri 10am–4pm; free; train: Flinders Street; map p.120 B4

Get the lowdown on the darker side of Victorian history by visiting this museum. Find out all about the colourful criminals who pounded the streets of Victoria and also the gallant work of the police force in such risky situations. Get to know 1870s detective John Christie, who was known as the force's Sherlock Holmes. And, if you've ever read about the

---

The **Koorie Heritage Trust** (295 King Street, corner of Little Lonsdale Street; tel: 03-8622 2600; www.koorieheritagetrust. com) is an Aboriginal community organisation that aims to protect, preserve and promote the living culture of Aboriginal people of southeastern Australia. It also has a collection of artefacts, paintings, photographs and written works, and uses the collections to promote the culture through a programme of permanent and temporary exhibitions on and offsite.

---

displays three generations of Chinese dragons.

Ian Potter Centre: NGV Australia

Federation Square, corner of Russell and Flinders Streets; tel: 03-8620 2222; www.ngv. vic.gov.au; daily 10am–5pm (closed Mon, Christmas Day and Boxing Day); free except for some exhibitions; train: Flinders Street; map p.121 D3

The home of Australian art presents Indigenous and non-Indigenous art from colonial times to the present. In fact, it has more Australian art on permanent display than any other gallery in the world. There are more than 20,000 works in the galleries, and about 800 of them are displayed at any one time, then rotated to show the real diversity of Australian art.

Immigration Museum

Old Customs House, 400 Flinders Street; tel: 13 11 02; museumvictoria.com.au; daily 10am–5pm (closed Good Friday and Christmas Day); charge for

---

Below: in the foyer of Melbourne Museum *(see p. 78)*.

famous Kelly gang, see their armour here. Also learn how forensic techniques are used, as well as finding out what Victoria Police is doing to make the state a safer place. With over 150 years of stories to tell, you won't be short of entertainment here. As the website says, 'To miss it would be a crime!'

CARLTON AND FITZROY
The Ian Potter Museum of Art

University of Melbourne, Swanston Street, between Faraday and Elgin Streets, Parkville; tel: 03-8344 5148; www.art-museum.unimelb.edu.au; Tue–Fri 10am–5pm, Sat–Sun noon–5pm; free; tram: number 1, 3, 5, 6, 8, 16, 64, 67, 72; map p.115 C2

This university art museum's building itself, with its striking design, is worth a look. It holds about 15 exhibitions a

year, and manages the university's art collection, which is the largest university collection in the country. Historic and contemporary paintings, decorative arts and sculpture are exhibited. It also has a strong representation of Australian art.

Melbourne Museum

11 Nicholson Street, Carlton; tel: 13 11 02; http://museum victoria.com.au; daily 10am–5pm (closed Good Friday and Christmas Day); charge for adults, free for children; train: Parliament, tram: 86, 96; map p.115 D2

Located in Carlton Gardens, this award-winning museum explores life in Victoria, with topics ranging from its natural environment to its culture and history. Check the website for a list of exhibitions during your time of visit. There are also several permanent

exhibitions, including the story of Sam the Koala, The Melbourne Story, Forest Secrets, CSIRAC – Australia's First Computer, and Phar Lap – a True Legend. Tours are available.

SOUTHBANK, DOCKLANDS, SOUTH WHARF AND SOUTH MELBOURNE
The Australian Centre for Contemporary Art

111 Sturt Street, Southbank; tel: 03-9697 9999; www.accaonline.org.au; Tue–Fri 10am–5pm, Sat–Sun 11am–6pm (closed Christmas Day and Good Friday); free; train: Flinders Street; map p.116 B2

Melbourne's leading contemporary art gallery showcases the most innovative visual art of our time. It brings in new and significant work from artists from around the world and also commissions new pieces from both local and international talents. The ACCA is not really considered as a museum, but follows the European tradition of the Kunsthalle, a German word that means 'exhibition hall'. Still, it's a large exhibition space that should be enjoyed by art fans.

Left: embrace the Aussie passion for sport at the National Sports Museum.

Above: exhibits at the Ian Potter Museum of Art.

[MARS]
Melbourne Art Rooms
418 Bay Street, Port Melbourne; tel: 03- 9681 8425; www.marsgallery.com.au; Tue–Sun 10am–5pm; charge; tram: 109

Also known as MARS Gallery, Melbourne Art Rooms has earned a reputation as one of the city's most exciting and diverse commercial art spaces. Opened in 2004, it's housed in a building that used to be an old dairy. It was neglected during its time as a warehouse and mechanical workshop, and this run-down look has been blended into its new incarnation too, offering a backdrop of simplicity and generous proportions. Works displayed here are by both emerging and established artists from Australia and around the world.

NGV International
180 St Kilda Road, Melbourne; tel: 03-8620 2222; www.ngv. vic.gov.au; Wed–Mon 10am–5pm (closed Christmas Day and Boxing Day); free except for some exhibitions; train: Flinders Street; map p.121 D4

The National Gallery of Victoria was founded in 1861 and is now split between two sites: at Federation Square you will find the Ian Potter Centre, which is dedicated to Australian art, while a short walk away, on St Kilda Road, you will find the international collection. Once you walk in, you will be greeted by the waterwall, a glass wall that's 20m (66ft) wide and 6m (20ft) high. Supporting a continually running, recycled water curtain, it was apparently built as a noise barrier between the very busy St Kilda Road and the much quieter gallery.

The other feature that NGV is known for is the Leonard French stained-glass ceiling in the Great Hall. It took five years to build and you are encouraged to get the best view by lying down on the ground, facing it. The gallery is known for its 'blockbuster' exhibitions and has hosted the works of Picasso and Salvador Dalí, as well as works from the Guggenheim.

SOUTH YARRA, PRAHRAN, RICHMOND AND TOORAK
National Sports Museum
Melbourne Cricket Ground, Brunton Avenue, Richmond; tel: 03-9657 8879; www.nsm. org.au; daily 10am–5pm (last admission 4pm, closed Good Friday and Christmas Day); charge; train: Jollimont, Richmond or Melbourne City Tourist Shuttle; map p.117 D1

Whether you are a sports fan or not, this museum makes an interesting trip, as it traces the history of Australian sport. Aptly, it's housed in the MCG, which is recognised by many as

79

Above: the Australian Centre for Contemporary Art *(see p.78)*.

If you are interested in art walks but want to do it at your own time and pace, drop by the Melbourne Visitor Centre at Federation Square, pick up a free Art Walk brochure and embark on a self-guided tour.

the home of Australian sport. Inside the museum, you'll find the Australian Gallery of Sport and Olympic Museum, Sport Australia Hall of Fame, Australian Cricket Hall of Fame, and the Australian Football exhibition, which includes the Hall of Fame. Tours are available, and it's a great way to find out just why this city is so obsessed with sports.
SEE ALSO SPORTS, P.102

AROUND THE BAY
Scienceworks and
Melbourne Planetarium
2 Booker Street, Spotswood; tel: 13 11 02; museumvictoria. com.au; daily 10am–4.30pm (closed Good Friday and Christmas Day); charge for adults, free for children; train: Spotswood
Scienceworks aims to present science and technology in unexpected and involving ways. There are live demonstrations,

guided tours, shows and other special activities. Exhibitions change regularly, so check the website for updated information.

Permanent exhibitions include Sportsworks, where you will learn all about the science behind moving your body, and House Secrets, an exploration of the science behind all the familiar things in our home. Melbourne Planetarium is housed within Scienceworks and allows visitors to enjoy the wonder of the stars no matter what the time of the day or the weather. Additional charges apply for shows at the planetarium.
SEE ALSO CHILDREN, P.41

Below: see fine art at the National Gallery of Victoria *(see p.79)*.

Above: take a Hidden Secrets Tour to see Melbourne's street art.

YARRA VALLEY AND DANDENONG RANGES
Heide Museum of Modern Art

7 Templestowe Road, Bulleen; tel: 03 9850 1500; www.heide. com.au; Tue–Sun 10am–5pm; charge; train: Heidelberg, then bus: 903 to Heide, disembark at Bridge Street

One of Australia's leading public art museums, Heide is located just 15 minutes from the CBD. It comprises 6.4 hectares (16 acres) of buildings, gardens and sculpture park, with a dramatic combination of indoor

Flinders Lane is a great place for art fans, as it has a large concentration of commercial galleries. Walk down this famous lane and you'll visit the studios of some of Melbourne's most exciting contemporary artists, as well as exhibitions of indigenous art from around the country.

and outdoor spaces. This unique space features modern and contemporary art and design, with a rich and colourful art heritage of social history. With various art spaces and even a café – Café Vue at Heide – this is one must-see venue for art fans.

ART WALKS AND TOURS
Hidden Secrets Tours

Tel: 03-9663 3358; www.hid densecretstours.com; Art and Design Walks most weekends

This company conducts walks to discover Melbourne's creative community. The most popular walk is the Lanes and Arcades Tour, which takes place Tue to Sat. The Art and Design Walks are held on most weekends, where you will get to take in some of the best public artworks on Melbourne's streets. Discover some hidden gems and then be able

to discuss art like a local afterwards.

Walk To Art

Tel: 03-8415 0449; www.walk toart.com.au; every Wed, Fri and Sat

Unearth hidden artistic gems in the heart of the Melbourne CBD. Walk To Art brings you to street art, art in artist-run spaces, art in galleries and in studios. It's a behind-the-scenes look at Melbourne's art community and an introduction to the world of art.

Guided by an art consultant, you will also get to talk to creators and art educators, and receive a 'starter pack' at the end of the tour, which will help you to further your art discovery. There's also a chance to chat about all the things you've seen, as you stop for wine and discussion at the end of the stroll.

Music

M usic in Melbourne is very much in the air you breathe. Whatever style or genre you prefer – whether rock, alternative, electronica, hip-hop, funk, world, classical, jazz, blues, folk or fusion – you can find some of the best exponents of it in formal concert venues, unconventional spaces and more atmospheric pubs and bars. There's a gig to catch in Melbourne almost every night, if you're not fussy about the genre of music. And it's possible to immerse yourself in a small gig with a few hundred watching or a stadium with about 50,000 singing along.

CLASSICAL

The **Melbourne Symphony Orchestra** (www.mso.com. au) performs at a variety of locations. In summer, usually in February, it performs its annual series of free concerts at the **Sidney Myer Music Bowl**.

The **Melbourne Chamber Orchestra** (www.mco. org.au) is the face of Australian chamber orchestral music. Founded in 1990, the orchestra comprises chamber ensembles and players of soloist calibre.

The **Royal Melbourne Philharmonic Orchestra** (www.rmp.org.au) has been presenting concerts for over 150 years and is Australia's oldest continuously existing musical organisation. It runs both a choir and an orchestra.

> Most radio stations have comprehensive gig guides. Recommended ones include the FM stations 3RRR (102.7 FM), 3MMM (105.1 FM) and 3PBS (106.7 FM). Try www.ausradio stations.com for links.

VENUES

The Arts Centre
100 St Kilda Road, Melbourne; tel: 1300 182 183; www.thearts centre.com.au; map p.121 D4
Popular venues here include State Theatre and Hammer Hall; the latter is closed for refurbishment until mid-2012. Outdoor venue Sidney Myer Music Bowl is great in summer, hosting artists as varied as Pearl Jam and Kiri Te Kanawa. SEE ALSO THEATRE AND DANCE, P.104

Melbourne Recital Centre
Corner of Southbank Boulevard and Sturt Street, Southbank; tel: 03-9699 2228; www.melbourne recital.com.au; bus: free Melbourne Tourist Shuttle; map p.121 D4
This venue is ranked among the world's great halls for its uncompromised acoustics. It has been recognised for its architecture and state-of-the-art facilities.

Melbourne Town Hall
Corner of Swanston and Collins streets, City Centre; tel: 03-9658

Above: conducting the Melbourne Symphony Orchestra.

9779; www.melbournetownhall. com.au; train: Flinders Street; map p.121 D2
The Beatles once graced this venue, which is home to a host of cultural and civic events.

JAZZ

The **Melbourne International Jazz Festival** (www.melbournejazz.com) is a popular annual event, held at venues across the city around May each year. The **Melbourne Jazz Fringe Festival** (melbournejazzfringe. com) consists of nine days and nights of creative and groundbreaking music.

Left: see live music any night of the week in Melbourne.

Sun 3pm–1am; train: Richmond; map p.117 D1
A grungy, cosy and easy place to be, with pool tables and a beer garden on the roof.

The Esplanade
11 The Esplanade, St Kilda; tel: 03-9534 0211; www.espy. com.au; Mon–Wed noon–1am, Thur noon–3am, Fri noon–3am, Sat 8am–3am, Sun noon–1am; tram: 16, 96; map p.119 C3
The 'Espy' is one of Melbourne's quintessential music venues. Bands play every night.

Hi-Fi Bar
125 Swanston Street, City Centre; tel: 1300 843 4434; www.thehifi.com.au; call for weekly set and door times; train: Flinders Street; map p.121 D2
One of the best live gig venues in the city, with a stream of of local and international acts. Located below street level.

Northcote Social Club
301 High Street, Northcote; tel: 03-9489 3917; www.north cotesocialclub.com; Mon 4pm–late, Tue–Thur noon–late, Fri–Sat noon–3am, Sun noon–late; train: Northcote; map p.119 E1
A respected music venue with folk, country, alternative, rock and fusions. The front bar is perfect to check out new bands, while the Deck is a beer garden.

Prince Bandroom
29 Fitzroy Street, St Kilda; tel: 03-9536 1168; www.princeband room.com.au; call for opening times; tram: 16; map p.119 C3
A host to live music for more than six decades, including Coldplay, Lenny Kravitz and Ben Harper.

JazzScene (www.jazzscene. com.au) is a monthly publication with details of jazz events all over Australia.

VENUES

Bennetts Lane Jazz Club
25 Bennetts Lane, City Centre, tel: 03-9663 2856; www.ben nettslane.com; daily 8.30pm– late (closed over Christmas/ New Year period); train: Melbourne Central; map p.121 D1
Melbourne's premier jazz venue, where high-calibre performances are the liturgy. Worth arriving early to make sure of a seat at this cosy and relaxed place.

Manchester Lane Jazz Club
234 Flinders Lane, City Centre; tel: 03-9663 0630; www.man chesterlane.com.au; Mon–Thur 5pm–late, Fri 11am–late, Sat 6pm–late; train: Flinders Street; map p.121 D3
Plush, trendy but intimate bar, with option of dinner near the stage; booking is essential. Monday is big bands, Fri–Sat soul and funk, with top Australian talent always moving through.

Tickets for pop and rock concerts especially sell very fast, so plan in advance and book early to avoid disappointment. Try Ticketek (www.ticketek. com.au) and TicketMaster (www.ticketmaster.com.au).

Paris Cat Jazz Club
6 Goldie Place, Melbourne; tel: 03-9642 4711; www.pariscat. com.au; Tue–Sun 5pm–late; train: Flinders Street or Melbourne Central; map p.120 C2
Cooler than cool, with a '30s French jazz ambience.

POPULAR
Melbourne's rock scene is based in pub venues. To see who's playing, grab the *Entertainment Guide* (EG) in *The Age* newspaper every Friday, or free weeklies *Inpres* and *Beat*.

VENUES

Corner Hotel
57 Swan Street, Richmond; tel: 03-9427 9198; www. cornerhotel.com; Rooftop Bar: Tue–Thur 4pm–late, Fri–Sun noon–late, Front Bar: Tue–Thur 4pm–late, Fri–Sat 2pm–3am,

Nightlife

Melbourne has a spectrum of nightclubs in the city centre that lure in party-goers every weekend. Many are underground venues or hidden in secluded spots, while others are perched on rooftops. A cardinal rule to remember: the cooler places are the more inconspicuous. For a great night out in the inner city, head to Brunswick Street, St Kilda or Prahran, which all have nightspots with resident and guest DJs. Some places open until dawn. In addition to dance clubs, Melbourne has a good choice of comedy and cabaret clubs. *See also Bars and Pubs, p.32, Gay and Lesbian, p.56 and Music, p. 82.*

THE CITY CENTRE

The Balcony

422 Little Collins Street; tel: 03-9642 8917; www.thebalcony.com.au; Fri 5pm–3am, Sat 9pm–3am; tram: 112; map p.120 C3

A sleek and sophisticated bar with a white leather quilted bar, white furnishings, pink fluorescent light and outdoor terrace with a glass enclosed balcony overlooking the street. Check out the line-up of DJs on weekends.

Ding Dong Lounge

Floor 1, 18 Market Lane; tel: 03-9662 1020; www.dingdonglounge.com.au; Wed–Thur 7pm–3am, Fri–Sat 7pm–7am; tram: 96; train: Parliament; map p.121 D2

Tucked away in the heart of Chinatown is Melbourne's underground and alternative rock 'n' roll bar, sister to New York City's Ding Dong Lounge. The club features DJs spinning a mix of classic and contemporary rock, new wave, electro, punk and garage.

Element Lounge

Lower Level, 85 Queen Street; tel: 03-9670 4880; www.elementlounge.com.au; Fri 9pm–3am, Sat 10pm–3am; tram: 112; map p.120 C3

Another underground venue, this spot is divided into five themes: water, wood, metal, fire and earth. Get your drinks at the 10m (33ft) long concrete bar, then hit the dancefloor and groove to house music by an excellent line-up of DJs.

Eleven A

11 Highlander Lane; tel: 03-9620 2228; Thur–Fri 4pm–1am, Sat 9pm–3am; tram: 75; train: Southern Cross; map p.120 B4

Located in the historic bluestone paved laneway, the refurbished Eleven A is one of the city's hippest boutique bar and nightclubs, with a large dancefloor. House, electro and funk are played most nights.

The Last Laugh Comedy Club

Athenaeum Theatre, 188 Collins Street, City Centre; tel: 03-9650 1977; www.thecomedyclub.com.au; tram: 112; map p.121 D2

The Last Laugh was the

Left: punters outside the Ding Dong Lounge.

Left: warming up for a night on the town.

terfly Club. Enjoy the show while sipping cocktails.

Fusion @ Crown
Level 3, Crown Entertainment Complex, 8 Whiteman Street; Southbank; tel 03-9292 5750; www.fusionatcrown.com.au; Thur 9.30pm–4am, Fri 9.30pm–4am, Sat 9.30pm–4am; train: Flinders Street or Southern Cross; map p.120 C4
A good mix of Aussie and international DJs spin the best R&B and house tunes. It also features three state-of-the-art bars and an exclusive VIP mezzanine.

After all the late-night partying, to get back to your accommodation, you can easily hop into a taxi or catch a NightRider bus – a safe, convenient and cheap mode of transport. Buses travel between the city (from City Square and Swanston Street) and suburbs, every 30 minutes between 1.30am–4.30am on Saturdays and 1.30am–5.30am on Sundays. There are more than 450 designated NightRider stops, but you can ask the driver to alight anywhere along the route, as long as it's safe to stop. For more information: www.metlinkmelbourne.com.au/timetables/nightrider.

birthplace of Melbourne's reputation as a comedy capital, and it is still going strong.

Sorry Grandma!
590–592 Little Bourke Street; tel: 03-9916 9029; www.sorrygrandma.com; Fri 10pm–8am, Sat 10pm–10 am; train: Southern Cross; map p.120 B3
Some of Melbourne's finest and longest-serving DJs play house and disco

at this two level club which opens way into the morning. Sip large-sized tea-based cocktails in the booth seats or head to the little nooks and crannies for more privacy.

CARLTON AND FITZROY
The Comic's Lounge
26 Errol Street, North Melbourne; tel: 03-9348 9488; www.thecomicslounge.com.au; dinner from 7pm, show from 8pm; tram: 57 from Elizabeth Street; map p.114 B3
Have a good laugh six nights a week at this lounge featuring a variety of stand-up comedians.

SOUTHBANK, DOCKLANDS, SOUTH WHARF AND SOUTH MELBOURNE
The Butterfly Club
204 Bank Street, South Melbourne; tel: 03-9690 2000; www.thebutterflyclub.com; nightly except Mon–Tue; tram: 1, 112; map p.116 B3
Housed in a Victorian shophouse, you will find cabaret, comedy and camp kitsch in equal measure at the But-

SOUTH YARRA, PRAHRAN, RICHMOND AND TOORAK
Revolver Upstairs
1st Floor, 229 Chapel Street, Prahran; www.revolverupstairs.com.au; tel: 03-9521 5985; Mon–Thur noon–4am, Fri–Sun 24hrs; tram: 78; map p.119 E1
Local and international DJs and bands are showcased here nightly. Look out too for record launches, indie film screenings and art exhibitions at this long-standing alternative venue.
SEE ALSO MARKETS, P.74

ST KILDA
George Lane Bar
1 George Lane (off Grey Street), St Kilda; tel: 03-9593 8884; www.georgelanebar.com.au; Tue–Sun 6pm–1am; tram 96; map p.119 D2
In a laneway behind the landmark George Hotel, this popular bar can't accommodate many drinkers, but those who do score a spot here always leave happy. There's a refreshingly laidback vibe and a DJ at weekends.

Parks and Gardens

Melbourne may be a buzzing city, but it's also possible to stop and smell the roses – or whatever your flower of choice. And you won't need to travel far to do this either, as there are various parks and gardens that are close to the city centre. Whether it's immaculate flowerbeds, exquisite sculptures or historic monuments that you're interested in, you will find them all in Melbourne's parks and gardens. Chill out with a book, meet friends for a picnic or take a kite and fly it. Whatever you choose to do, it's easy to find a spot to feel relaxed or simply soak up the Australian sun.

ALBERT PARK

Albert Road, Albert Park; tel: 03-9695 9000; www.parkweb. vic.gov.au; tram: 96, 112; map p.116 B4

Located in the city of Port Phillip, around 3km (2 miles) from the CBD, Albert Park boasts a picturesque lake and a network of trails. It's a sporting and recreational park that is also an important sanctuary for wildlife and vegetation. Have a picnic or barbecue, walk around the lake and see the swans, or just take

your bike for a cycle. Several sporting events are held year throughout the year, the most famous being the Formula One Australian Grand Prix. There's also a golf course and restaurants, and on-water activities such as rowing are possible too.
SEE ALSO SPORTS, P.101

CARLTON GARDENS

Victoria Parade, Carlton and Nicholson Streets, Carlton; tel: 03-9658 9658; http://museum victoria.com.au/reb/history/ carlton-gardens/; daily 10am– 10pm; train: Parliament or free City Circle Tram; map p.115 D2

This is where you should go to get a brilliant example of Victorian-era landscape design. With sweeping lawns and European and Australian trees, it's the perfect place for a stroll, with the likes of stunning lakes, beautiful flowerbeds and fountains to enjoy too. The Gardens are also home to the Royal Exhibition Building, which was built for the Great Exhibition of 1880. The building and gardens

Above: Cook's Cottage.

were both added to the World Heritage List in 2004. Carlton Gardens also house the Melbourne Museum, IMAX Cinema, tennis courts and a playground.
SEE ALSO MUSEUMS AND GALLERIES, P.78

FITZROY GARDENS

230–298 Wellington Parade, East Melbourne; tel: 03-9658 9658; Cook's Cottage and Conservatory: daily 9am–5pm; www.fitzroygardens.com; tram: 48, 75; map p.115 E3

Melbourne is one of the few cities that has such a significant garden so close to the city centre. The garden

Melbourne's first public garden was Flagstaff Gardens. It was established on the highest point of land in the city and hosted a signalling station, which is still there. It was known as Burial Hill, as it was a burial site before Melbourne Cemetery was established. Today, it's a popular lunchtime spot for people working in the city's northwest and has picnic and barbecue areas, a walking path, as well as netball, tennis and volleyball courts. The nearest station is Flagstaff.

Left: the Royal Exhibition Building in Carlton Gardens.

flora, roses, herbs, succulents, as well as plants from southern China. It's also a natural sanctuary for native wildlife such as black swans, cockatoos and kookaburras. During the warmer months, the gardens plays host to film screenings, theatre performances and markets, the most popular being the Moonlight Cinema. There are a number of walks and tours that you can join. Don't forget to pick up a souvenir at the Gardens Shop on your way out.
SEE ALSO FILM, P.51

has a history of more than 150 years and is visited by over 2 million visitors annually. Cook's Cottage is a must see, a memorial to Captain James Cook, who discovered the east cost of Australia. There's also a Conservatory, a vital part of the city's commitment to horticulture. Tudor Village is another great attraction, and look out for the variety of sculptures scattered all over the gardens.

QUEEN VICTORIA GARDENS

St Kilda Road, City Centre; tel: 03-0658 9658; tram: any southbound tram from Flinders Street, except 1 or 2; map p.1212 D4
A favourite spot for wedding photographs, this is must-see for lovers of flowers. Walk through impeccably maintained beds of annuals and roses or just pose by the giant floral clock, which is made up of about 7,000 flowers and has been in the gardens since 1966. Look out for the many sculptures dotted all over the gardens

or just enjoy the waterlilies that fill the pond.

ROYAL BOTANIC GARDENS

Visitor Centre, Observatory Gate, Birdwood Avenue, South Yarra; tel: 03-9252 2412; www.rbg.vic.gov.au; daily 7.30am–sunset; bus: free Melbourne City Tourist Shuttle; map p.117 D2
Extending over 36 hectares (90 acres) and attracting over 1.6 million visitors each year, the Royal Botanic Gardens have a reputation as one of the finest gardens in the world. You'll find some amazing plant collections here, such as camellias, rainforest

ROYAL PARK

Flemington Road, Parkville; tel: 03-9658 9658; train: Royal Park; map p.114 B1
Royal Park covers 180 hectares (450 acres) and sits about 2km (1¼ miles) north of the city centre. It's best known as the home of Melbourne Zoo. If large open spaces are your thing, this is the place for you. It is perfect for a relaxing walk or to park yourself under a tree with a book. There's also a garden of Australian native plants and Urban Camp, remnants of an army base from World War II.
SEE ALSO CHILDREN, P.41

Below: several statues are found in Queen Victoria Gardens.

Restaurants

Melbourne is undeniably a city for food-lovers. Many internationally renowned chefs have set up here over the past few years, elevating the culinary scene yet further. Foodies also continue to flock to stalwarts that are quintessentially Australian, helmed by home-grown talents. The city also offers a melting pot of cuisines that suits every taste and budget. Most standout places are found in the city centre or inner suburbs, with other hotspots being Southbank, Fitzroy and St Kilda. Fine wine lists are often available for perfect pairings. The restaurants listed are all popular, so reservations are highly recommended.

THE CITY CENTRE

Becco

11–25 Crossley Street; tel: 03-9663 3000; www.becco.com.au; Mon–Sat noon–3pm and 6–11pm; $$$; train: Parliament; map p.121 D2

This stylish Italian restaurant-bar is tucked down a laneway at the eastern end of Bourke Street. City residents come to enjoy the home-style Italian cooking, including pasta classics and comfort mains such as *cotoletta* (crumbed veal cutlet). The bar serves inexpensive lunches during the day and tasty bar snacks at night.

Cookie

Level 1, 252 Swanston Street; tel: 03-9663 7660; www.cookie.net.au; daily noon–11pm (bar noon–3am); $; tram

Prices for a three-course dinner per person with a glass of house wine:
$ = below A$60
$$ = A$60–90
$$$ = A$90–120
$$$$ = over A$120

1, 3, 3a; map p.121 C2

Boho Melbourne loves to drink at this excellent bar, and those in the know also eat their fill at Cookie's funky restaurant, where the inventive and tasty Thai fusion cuisine pleases both palate and wallet.

Cumulus Inc.

45 Flinders Lane; tel: 03-9650 1445; www.cumulusinc.com.au; Mon–Fri 7am–11pm, Sat–Sun 8am–11pm; $; tram: 75; map p.121 E2

This light-filled casual chic venue by Chef Andrew

Below: in Jamie Oliver's Fifteen Melbourne.

McConnell of the famed Cutler & Co. serves fresh Mediterranean-style fare from light salads to hearty charcuterie and robust braises for lunch and dinner. It is usually packed with business executives, so get there before the lunch crowds arrive. Healthy breakfast items are offered too.

European

161 Spring Street; tel: 03-9654 0811; www.theeuropean.com.au; daily 7.30am–3am; $$; train: Parliament; tram: 48; map p.121 E1

An all-European wine list, reliable European bistro favourites, excellent coffee, old-world wood-panelled dining room and efficient service topped with a 3am closing time have made this dining venue a favourite, especially among the theatre crowd.

ezard

187 Flinders Lane: tel: 03-9639 6811; www.ezard.com.au; Mon–Fri noon–2.30pm, 6pm–late, Sat 6pm–late; $$$$; train:

Left: top-notch fare at Monalto *(see p.94)*.

New World labels that harmonise well with the boldly flavoured dishes.

Grossi Florentino

80 Bourke Street, tel: 03-9662 1811; www.grossiflorentino. com; Mon–Sat 7.30pm–late; $$$$; train: Parliament; map p.121 D2

This Melbourne Italian institution, which has been around for over 75 years, is three businesses in one, the grand and expensive upstairs restaurant, the 1960s glamorous Grill and the stylishly bohemian, wood-panelled Cellar Bar, popular among the pre-theatre crowd.

Kenzan

Collins Place, 45 Collins Street; tel: 03-9654 8933; www.kenzan. com.au; Mon–Fri noon–2.15pm, Mon–Sat 6pm–10pm; $$; train: Flinders Street; tram: 112; map p.121 E2

The 27-year-old Kenzan was one of the first Japanese restaurants in Melbourne and has remained among the best. Sushi and sashimi are excellent, and the specials list is always interesting.

Below: the hugely popular Longrain *(see p.90)*.

Restaurants do not usually include service charges. Although tipping is not obligatory, it is becoming more common to tip waiters up to 10 percent of the bill for good service.

Flinders Street; map p.121 D3

The sophisticated decor of this restaurant in the basement of the Adelphi Hotel is more than matched by the menu, featuring stunningly presented and skilfully executed dishes. Owner-chef Teague Ezard uses the finest local produce for his dishes, which are influenced by Chinese, Thai and a sprinkling of Middle Eastern flavours.

Fifteen Melbourne

Basement, 115–117 Collins Street; tel: 1-300 799 415; www.fifteenmelbourne.com.au; Mon–Sat noon–3pm, Mon–Sun 6pm–10pm; $$$; tram: 112; map p.121 D2

Antipodean offspring of Jamie Oliver's Fifteen in the UK, the Melbourne restaurant has the same charitable underpinning with rustic Italian influenced seasonal cuisine. Watch chefs cooking up a storm in the open kitchen and enjoy the buzzing atmosphere.

Flower Drum

17 Market Lane; tel: 03-9662 3655; www.flower-drum.com; Mon–Sat noon–3pm, 6pm–11pm, Sun 6pm–10.30pm; $$$; tram: 96; map p.121 D2

Considered one of the best fine dining Cantonese restaurants in Australia, Flower Drum, which opened in 1975, continues to offer well-executed meals, expert service and an undeniable sense of occasion.

Gingerboy

27–29 Crossley Street; tel: 03-9662 4200; www.gingerboy. com.au; Mon–Fri noon–2.30pm, Mon–Sat 6pm–late; $$; train: Parliament; map p.121 D2

Southeast Asian hawker food gets a designer makeover here, complete with excellent cocktails and a wine list of Old and

Longrain

44 Little Bourke Street; tel: 03-9671 3151; www.longrain. com.au; Fri noon–3pm, Mon–Fri 6pm–11pm, Sat–Sun 5.30pm–11pm; $$$; train: Parliament; map p.121 D1

An outpost of the famous Sydney establishment, serving modern Thai-inspired cuisine. In a huge warehouse-style space in Chinatown, Longrain's long and round communal tables are inevitably full of glamorous young things sharing a spicy meal together.

MoVida

1 Hosier Lane; tel: 03-9663 3038; www.movida.com.au; daily noon–late; $$–$$$; train: Flinders Street; map p.121 D3

One of the city's favourite tapas restaurants, MoVida looks to Madrid for inspiration. Owner-chef Frank Camorra trained in Spain and delivers assured tapas and raciones, utilising a mix of top-quality local produce and the best Iberian imports. Dishes range from classic to unexpected, and are consistently delicious. No luck scoring a table? Try **MoVida Next Door** (Corner of Flinders Street and Hosier Lane; Fri–Sat noon–midnight, Tue–Thur 5pm–late; $$) or the

newer and larger **MoVida Aqui** (Level 1, 500 Bourke Street, Mon–Fri noon until late, Sat 5pm until late; $$; tram: 86, 96).

The Press Club

72 Flinders Street; tel: 03-9677 9677; www.thepressclub. com.au; Mon–Sat noon–3pm, Mon–Sun 6pm–10pm, Kerasma Lunch: Sun 11.30am–3pm; $$$$; train: Flinders Street, tram: 48,75; map p.121 E2

Celebrity chef George Calombaris, who's often seen on the wildly popular *Masterchef* TV show, runs this place housed in the old Herald and Weekly Times Building. Contemporary Greek cuisine concocted using modern techniques and the finest ingredients are presented. The eight-course Symposium dégustation menu paired with wines is highly recommended.

Sarti

6 Russell Place; tel: 03-9639 7822; www.sarti.net.au; Mon–Fri noon–3pm, Mon–Sat 6pm–10.30pm; $$$; tram: 96; map p.121 D2

The menu here has a classic Italian base but features some intriguing modern twists. The *stuz-*

The dress code is generally smart and elegant rather than formal for fine dining restaurants. Some places draw the line at customers wearing tank tops, ripped jeans or flip-flops.

zichini (small appetisers designed to be shared) are full of fun and flavour, and the mains inevitably incorporate an unusual ingredient or two. Best of all are the sublime desserts. The rooftop terrace offers a great place to chill out.

Society

23 Bourke Street; 03-9639 2544; www.societyrestaurant. com; Mon–Fri 7am–10pm, Sat 9am–10pm; $$; tram: 96; map p.121 D2

The 80-year-old Society continues to attract a crowd with its flavoursome homespun Italian food. The current owners carefully restored the venue, bringing back the glory days when this was the former hangout of the 'spaghetti mafia', a close-knit group of passionate Italian restaurateurs.

Supper Inn

15 Celestial Avenue; tel: 03-9663 4759; daily 5.30pm–2.30am; $; tram: 1, 3, 6; map p.121 D2

Another 'institution' in the city. Always crowded (particularly late at night), it has a no-frills decor, abrupt service and utterly wonderful Cantonese food (think: suckling pig and spicy quail).

Taxi Dining Room

Level 1, Transport Hotel, Federation Square; www.trans

Left: airy space in the Taxi Dining Room.

Right: visit the Hellenic Republic for excellent Greek food *(see p.92)*.

porthotel.com.au; tel: 03-9654 8808; daily noon–3pm and 6pm–late; $$$$; train: Flinders Street; map p.121 D3

Locals wanting to impress clients or first dates head toward this Japanese-accented restaurant in Federation Square. Executive chef Michael Lambie trained with Marco Pierre White, and his impressive creations are complemented by an extraordinarily fine wine list.

Vue de Monde

430 Little Collins Street; tel: 03-9691 3888; www.vue demonde.com.au; Tue–Fri noon–2pm, Tue–Sat 6.30pm–8.30pm; $$$$; tram: 112; map p.120 C3

One of Australia's finest restaurants, Shannon Bennett's Vue de Monde at the historic Normanby Chambers is not for diners after a low-key meal. The dégustation menu served in the evening is exquisite, topped with a hint of humour. The daily set-lunch deal offers a more affordable taste of Bennett's cuisine, as does the menu at adjoining **Bistro Vue** (tel: 03-9691 3838; Mon–Sat 11am–late; $$).

Yu-u

137 Flinders Lane; tel: 03-9639 7073; Mon–Fri noon–2.15pm, Mon–Sat 6pm–9.30pm; $; train: Flinders Street, tram: 48, 75; map p.121 D2

Located in a rather obscure spot, this basement Japanese restaurant with no obvious signage has attracted many fans that come here for its modern Japanese menu.

EAST MELBOURNE

Verge

1 Flinders Lane; tel: 03-9639 9500; www.vergerestaurant. com.au; Mon–Sat noon–3pm, 6pm–10.30pm; $$$; train: Parliament; map p.121 E2

Edgy modern decor, including a 'glass box' dining room overlooking the lush Treasury Gardens, echoes the modernity of its cooking injected with some Japanese, French and Mediterranean influences.

CARLTON AND FITZROY

Abla's

109 Elgin Street, Carlton; tel: 03-9347 0006; www.ablas. com.au; Thur–Fri noon–3pm, Mon–Sat 6pm–11pm; $; tram: 96; map p.115 D2

Abla Amad's delectable home-style Lebanese food has devotees throughout the city. The kibbe and kebabs are delicious, and the spiced pilaf with minced lamb, chicken and almonds is to die for.

Balzari

130 Lygon Street, Carlton; tel: 03-9639 9383; www.balzari. com.au; Tue–Fri noon–late, Sat–Sun 9.30am–late; $$; tram: 1, 8; map p.115 D2

Balzari is a haven of style and good food wedged among the tatty tourist restaurants of Lygon Street.

The menu takes inspiration from northern Italy.

Cutler & Co.

55–57 Gertrude Street; tel: 03-9419 4888; www. cutlerandco.com.au; Tue–Sun 6pm–late, Sun noon–3pm; $$–$$$; tram: 112, 86; map p.115 E3

This highly acclaimed restaurant by Andrew McConnell has received rave reviews from critics for its wow factor. The space of an old metalwork factory was transformed into the stylish dining room and bar. And the food perfectly balanced in taste and texture is simple, fresh and fabulous.

Gigibaba

102 Smith Street, Collingwood; tel: 03-9486 0345; Tue–Sun 6–11pm; $; tram: 86; map p.115 E2

Ismail Tosun's modern takes on Turkish classics have the city's foodie fraternity frantically queuing for tables (there's a no-booking policy). His tapas-style

Prices for a three-course dinner per person with a glass of house wine:
$ = below A$60
$$ = A$60–90
$$$ = A$90–120
$$$$ = over A$120

91

should have put off some of the city's notoriously fickle foodies, but even this hasn't stopped the crowds flocking to this huge and theatrical Italian eatery at the Crown Casino. The menu features classic Roman dishes including lots of meat items, and the wine list includes lots of well-priced Italian choices.

dishes are sure to appeal to all palates, and the stylish fit-out provides a funky feel.

Hellenic Republic

434 Lygon Street, Brunswick East; tel: 03-9381 1222; www. hellenicrepublic.com.au; Sat–Sun 9am–11.30am, Fri–Sun noon–4pm, Mon–Sun 5.30pm–late; $; tram: 1, 8; map p.115 D1
This taverna is owned by high-profile chef George Calombaris of Press Club fame, and is characterised by a casual atmosphere and a traditional Greek tavern cuisine with a fresh twist, and using only the freshest ingredients. Robust Greek wine is served by the litre.

Ladro

224 Gertrude Street, Fitzroy; tel: 03-9415 7575; Tue–Sun 6–11pm, Sun noon–3pm; $; tram: 112, 86; map p.115 E3
Melbourne's best pizza is on offer at this bustling place. In winter the roasted meat of the day is popular, but what the punters mainly come for are the thin-crust pizzas topped with delights such as potato and truffle oil.

Pireaus Blues

310 Brunswick Street, Fitzroy; tel: 03-9417 0222; www.

pireausblues.com.au; Wed–Sat noon-3pm, Mon–Sat 5pm– late, Sun noon–late, $$; tram: 112; map p.115 E1
This lively spot serves traditional Greek staples from the north to the Mediterranean. Feast on the most delicious chargrilled meats and seafood alongside fresh salads.

SOUTHBANK, DOCKLANDS, SOUTH WHARF AND SOUTH MELBOURNE

Bhoj Docklands

54 Promenade, New Quay, Docklands; tel: 03-9600 0884; www.bhoj.com.au; daily noon–3pm, 5.30pm–10.30pm; $$; train: Southern Cross, the Melbourne City Tourist Shuttle; map p.114 B4
Melbourne's smartest Indian restaurant is also one of its best, with deftly cooked dishes from across the subcontinent, and a wine list complete with food-matching guidelines for Indian food.

Giuseppe Arnaldo & Sons

Crown Complex, 8 Whiteman Street, Southbank; tel: 03-9694 7400; www.idrb.com; daily noon–midnight; $$; train: Flinders Street or Southern Cross; map p.120 C4
The no-booking policy

Maze Melbourne

Level 1, Crown Metropol, Corner of Whiteman and Clarendon Streets, Southbank; tel: 03-9292 8300; www. gordonramsay.com/australian restaurants; Mon–Sun 6.30am–10.30am, noon–2.30pm, 6pm–11pm; $$; train: Flinders Street; map p.116 A2
With celebrity chefs like Nobu and Jamie Oliver launching restaurants in this city, it didn't take long for British culinary maestro Gordon Ramsay to jump on the bandwagon. His first Australian restaurants, Maze and Maze Grill, highlight the freshest and finest seasonal ingredients available throughout Australia. The items are presented on tasting-sized plates, so diners can order individually or sample multiple dishes.

Melbourne has many food festivals and events that lure in foodies from everywhere. The most famous is the Melbourne Food and Wine Festival, whose programme boasts over 300 food and wine events across Victoria. Held in March, the festival also shines the spotlight on guest chefs and top winemakers from overseas.

Nobu Melbourne

Crown Complex, 8 Whiteman Street, Southbank; tel: 03-9292 7879; Mon–Thur noon–2.30pm, Fri–Sun noon–3pm, Sun–Thur 6pm–10.30pm, Fri–Sat 6pm–11pm; $$$$; train: Flinders Street or Southern Cross; map p.116 A2

Nobu's Southern Hemisphere outpost, just like the rest of this culinary empire, is a glamorous and vibrant affair. The modern Japanese menu follows the Nobu formula of great ingredients and flavours. Look out for the signature black cod with miso.

O'Connell's

407 Coventry Street, South Melbourne; tel: 03-9699 9600; www.oconnells.com.au; daily noon–3pm, 6pm–11pm; $$; tram: 112; map p.116 A3

Set in a leafy backstreet, O'Connell's has been impressing with its Modern European comfort fare for about 16 years.

Red Emperor

Upper Level, 3 Southgate Avenue, Southbank; tel: 03-9699 4170; www.redemperor.com.au; Mon–Sat noon–3pm, Sun 11am–4pm; $$$; train: Flinders Street; map p.121 D4

This large, loud Chinese restaurant has great city views, excellent service and some of the best dim sum in town.

Rockpool Bar & Grill

Crown Complex, 8 Whiteman Street, Southbank; tel: 03-8648 1900; www.rockpool.com; Sun–Fri noon–3pm, daily 6pm–11pm; $$$$; train: Flinders Street or Southern Cross; map p.116 A2

This restaurant by the famous Aussie chef Neil Perry is fashioned after American steakhouses.

Prices for a three-course dinner per person with a glass of house wine:
$ = below A$60
$$ = A$60–90
$$$ = A$90–120
$$$$ = over A$120

The beef is sourced from Australia's best producers and dry-aged on the premises, so diners are assured of the best quality. There is exquisitely fresh seafood to be had too.

Tutto Bene

Mid-level, Southgate, Southbank; tel: 03-9696 3334; daily noon–3pm, 6pm–late; $$; train: Flinders Street; map p.121 D4

A down-to-earth Italian joint with a balcony overlooking the Yarra River. Being Melbourne's only risotteria, the risotto prepared by a master risotto chef is recommended, as are the rustic meat dishes and house-made gelati.

SOUTH YARRA, PRAHRAN, RICHMOND AND TOORAK

Bacash

175 Domain Road, South Yarra; tel: 03-9866 3566; www.bacash.com.au; Mon–Fri noon–3pm, Mon–Sat 6pm–10pm; $$$; tram: 8; map p.117 D3

This nicely appointed parkside restaurant is only a short walk from the Botanical Gardens. Seafood is the main event and includes oysters, sashimi-grade yellow fin tuna, scallops and other fresh catches.

The Botanical

169 Domain Road, South Yarra, tel: 03-9820 7888; www.thebotanical.com.au; Mon–Fri 7am–3pm, 6pm–11.30pm, Sat–Sun 8am–3pm, 6pm–11.30pm; $$–$$$; tram: 8; map p.117 D3

Located on a leafy road overlooking the Botanic Gardens is the famous Botanical. Superb contemporary food from breakfast to nightcap attracts a crowd interested in substance as much as style. Check out the bottle shop at the entrance.

Da Noi

95 Toorak Road, South Yarra; tel: 03-9866 5975; Tue–Sat noon–3pm, Mon–Sat 6pm–10pm; $$$; tram: 8; map p.117 D3

Native Sardinian Pietro Porcu creates memorable dishes for his many fans. There is a menu at this rustically decorated, Sardinian influenced restaurant, but nobody

Below: tuck into steak at Rockpool Bar & Grill.

uses it. Instead they opt for the Chef's Choice and let the kitchen make the call, saving decision-making for the all-Italian wine list.

France-Soir

11 Toorak Road, South Yarra; tel: 03-9866 8569; www.france-soir.com.au; daily noon–3pm, 6pm–midnight; $$$; tram: 8; map p.117 D3

France-Soir has kept going for more than 20 years thanks to its consistently good-quality French bistro favourites and an award-winning French-leaning wine list. It also specialises in pre-theatre dinners and late suppers.

Jacques Reymond

78 Williams Road, Windsor; tel: 03-9525 2178; www.jacquesreymond.com.au; Thur–Fri noon–1.30pm, Tue–Sat 6.30pm–9.30pm; $$$$; tram: 78

Gourmands are drawn to the restrained elegance and sophisticated execution of dishes crafted by Jacques Reymond, one of the most innovative and exciting chefs in Australia. Housed in a suburban 1880s mansion, the restaurant has been consistently awarded three chef hats (see p.54) and many other accolades.

Pearl

631–633 Church Street, Richmond; tel: 03-9421 4599; www.pearlrestaurant.com.au; daily noon–3pm, 6pm–11pm; $$$$; tram: 79; map p.117 D2

Brilliantly inventive food, much of it borrowing flavour and technique from Southeast Asia, perfectly matched by smooth service, a sleekly comfortable room and a noteworthy wine selection.

ST KILDA
Circa, The Prince

2 Acland Street; tel: 03-9536 1122; www.circa.com.au; daily 7am–11am, 6pm–10pm, Fri noon–2pm, Sun 12.30–2.30pm; $$$$; tram: 16, 96; map p.119 C3

One of Melbourne's most romantically stylish dining rooms also boasts some elegant and innovative dishes featuring quality seasonal produce and organic heirlooms. The chefs take their food so seriously, they even have a working kitchen garden.

Donovans

40 Jacka Boulevard; tel: 03-9534 8221; www.donovanshouse.com.au; daily noon–10.30pm; $$$–$$$$, tram 16; map p.119 C3

Donovans just by the beach combines bayside breeziness with an assured but conservative Italian menu heavy on seafood options. The views of St Kilda beach are fabulous, the terrace is a wonderful spot for lunch, and the 'cubby house' menu for kids is a great innovation.

Stokehouse

30 Jacka Boulevard; tel: 03-9525 5555; www.stokehouse.com.au; daily noon–2.30pm and 6–10pm; $$–$$$$; tram: 16; map p.119 C3

Set in a beautifully restored beachside house, this is one of the first ports of call when Melburnians want to impress visitors from out of town. The downstairs bar serves casual fare like fish and chips, and the upstairs restaurant, which has a balcony with a superb view of the bay, offers a sophisticated, well-thought-out Mediterranean-inspired menu.

AROUND THE BAY
Montalto

33 Shoreham Road, Red Hill South; tel: 03-5989 8412; www.montalto.com.au; daily noon–3pm, Fri–Sat 6.30pm–11pm (in summer, also Mon–Thur 6pm–9pm); $$–$$$; hire a car

The fabulous views from the glass-and-timber building, landscaped gardens full of sculpture, picnic areas and regional French-

Right: the Healesville Hotel is great for local produce.

style dishes favouring local produce make this one of the Mornington Peninsula's best picks.

Queenscliff Hotel
16 Gellibrand Street, Queenscliff; tel: 03-5258 1066; www.queenscliffhotel.com.au; daily noon–3pm, 6–9pm; $$$; hire a car

This grand old 1887 Victorian hotel is not only big on nostalgic atmospherics but also serves up decent food in its sheltered courtyard and grand candlelit dining room.

YARRA VALLEY AND DANDENONG RANGES
Eleonore's Restaurant
42 Melba Highway, Yering, Yarra Valley; tel: 03-9237 3333; daily 6.30pm–late, Sat–Sun noon–3pm; www.chatcauyering.com.au; $$$–$$$$; hire a car

One of the finest restaurants in Yarra Valley is Eleonore's, located at the historic five-star hotel Chateau Yering. Executive Chef Mathew Macartney ensures that the dining experience is a memorable one – his contemporary creations using seasonal produce are paired with an extensive selection of Yarra Valley wines.

Healesville Hotel Dining Room
256 Maroondah Highway, Healesville; tel: 03-5962 4002; www.healesvillehotel.com.au; Wed–Sun noon–3pm, 6pm–9pm; $$; train: Lilydale, then bus 685 or 686 to Healesville

Located in the 1910 Healesville Hotel is this

beautiful restaurant with an old-world ambience and a courtyard. The menu features a superb selection of local produce such as yabbies, oysters and free-range pork.

Locale
De Bortoli Winery, 58 Pinnacle Lane, Dixons Creek; tel: 03-5965 2271; www.debortoliyarra.com.au; Thur–Mon noon–2.30pm, Sat 6.30–8.30pm; $$; hire a car

This winery restaurant is the place to linger after a meal and enjoy glasses of excellent estate wine. The chef commissions local farmers to grow special heirloom Italian produce exclusively for the restaurant. Many of the vegetables and herbs are grown in the kitchen garden too, so only the freshest are served.

GREAT OCEAN ROAD
Chris's Restaurant
280 Skenes Creek Road, Apollo Bay; tel: 03-5237 641; www.chriss.com.au; daily 8.30am–10am, noon–2pm, 6pm–10pm; $$$; hire a car

It may be a tad tricky to find this restaurant perched on a hilltop high in

the Otways, but the drive up is well worth the effort. The chef makes the most of his Greek background, and places emphasis on fresh local seafood to corner the top end of the market. Wherever you are seated, you will be rewarded with stunning views of the surroundings.

Pippies by the Bay
Flagstaff Hill, 89 Merri Street, Warrnambool; tel: 03-5561 2188; Mon–Fri 12pm–2.30pm, 6pm–8.30pm, Sat–Sun 10am–8pm (June–Aug closed for Sun dinner and Mon); $$; hire a car

Seasonally driven Italian-style dishes, many of them using locally sourced produce, are worthy competitors to the beautiful view of tranquil Lady Bay. Combine a 'Shipwrecked' dinner and laser show package with Flagstaff Hill.

Prices for a three-course dinner per person with a glass of house wine:
$ = below A$60
$$ = A$60–90
$$$ = A$90–120
$$$$ = over A$120

Left: Stokehouse's balcony is perfect for alfresco dining.

95

Shopping

Melburnians love their retail therapy and have taken shopping seriously for a long time, as evidenced by the beautiful 19th-century arcades and Collins Street's 'Paris End'. Every shopping precinct in the CBD and city fringe is distinctive – whether Bourke Street Mall for grand department stores, Flinders Lane for local designers' latest creations, Richmond for factory outlets, or Fitzroy for alternative style and retro fashions. Over in South Yarra, Chapel Street and Toorak Road, the well-heeled frequent the many designer boutiques. *See also Fashion, p.46, Food and Drink, p.52, Literature, p.70 and Markets, p.72.*

SHOPPING PRECINCTS

Bourke Street Mall, right in the heart of the city, is home to the Myer and David Jones department stores as well as the fashionable GPO (refurbished Post Office). Within walking distance are the Melbourne Central, with its multilevel glass atrium, and QV shopping centres, which house numerous mid- to high-end boutiques.

The small designer boutiques clustered in the city's laneways and arcades are worth exploring, especially for unique one-off pieces. Little Collins Street is lined with local designer boutiques, and Flinders Lane is the place to find trendy Australian-designed jewellery and handmade accessories. On the main thoroughfare of Collins Street, you will find high-end stores such as Tiffany, Chanel and Louis Vuitton.

Accessories, toiletries, funky homeware as well as alternative and vin-

Shopping Secrets (www. shoppingsecrets.com) is an innovative shopping guide to Melbourne in a compact deck of cards. Each card includes a description of a store and a map of its location. Available from good bookstores.

tage fashion are strongly represented in Fitzroy's Gertrude and Brunswick Streets. The weekend Rose Street Market is a venue where local designers get to showcase their handcrafted products here.

Chapel Street in South Yarra is lined with local fashion labels Bettina Liano, Alannah Hill, Collette Dinnigan, Metalicus and Scanlan & Theodore. Travel south into Windsor to find the funky Chapel Street Bazaar, home to vintage furniture and bric-a-brac. SEE ALSO FASHION, P.46; MARKETS, P.74

BEAUTY AND SKINCARE

Aesop

Shop 1C, 284 Flinders Lane; tel: 03-9663 0862; www.aesop. net.au; Mon–Sat 10am–6pm, Sun noon–5pm; train: Flinders Street; map p.121 C3

Launched in Melbourne in 1987, this renowned brand has since expanded globally. Aesop is known for its natural skin, hair and body products made from the highest quality plant-based ingredients and other elements such as antioxidants.

Kleins Perfumery

313 Brunswick Street, Fitzroy; tel: 03-9416 1221; www. kleinsperfumery.com.au; Mon–Thur 9.30am–6.30pm, Fri 9am–9pm, Sat 9am–6.30pm, Sun 10am–6pm; tram: 112; map p.115 E1

Established in 1993, this tiny store houses over 80 different brands. It specialises in niche fragrances sourced from perfume houses worldwide, as well as Australian-made skincare and haircare. There are home fragrances like candles, drawer liners and incense, as well as handmade soap – perfect for gifts.

Left: the old Melbourne GPO has been converted into a shopping centre *(see p.99).*

something to match with any outfit of yours.

City Hatters

211 Flinders Street; tel: 03-9614 3294; www.cityhatters.com.au; train: Flinders Street; map p.121 D3

The renowned century-old City Hatters in Flinders Street Station is the place to go for all manner of headgear – from berets to caps, formal and outback hats. It carries a range of brands including the famous Akubra. You are bound to find a hat for any occasion in this store.

Counter

31 Flinders Lane; tel: 03-9650 7775; www.craftvic.asn.au; Mon–Sat, 10am–5pm; train: Flinders Street; tram: 75; map p.121 E2

Stylish handmade items crowd the shelves at Counter, the retail arm of Craft Victoria. Artisans sell one-off pieces of jewellery, glass, ceramics, homewares and others – most

DEPARTMENT STORES

David Jones

310 Bourke Street Mall; tel: 03-9643 2222; www.davidjones.com.au; Mon–Wed 9.30am–7pm, Thur–Fri 9.30am–9pm, Sat 9am–7pm, Sun 10am–7pm; tram: 86, 96; map p.121 C2

Just opposite Myer is David Jones. This store underwent a major renovation recently and now houses high-end brands such as Miu Miu, Tods, Burberry, Coach and many others.

Myer

314 Bourke Street Mall/ 295 Lonsdale Street; tel: 03-9661 1111; www.myer.com.au; Mon–Wed 9am–7pm, Thur 9am–8pm, Fri 9am–9pm, Sat 9am–7pm, Sun 10am–7pm; tram: 86, 96; map p.121 C2

The newly refurbished department store is the place to find just about anything from fashion and cosmetics to homeware. Check out the Christmas window display.

JEWELLERY AND ACCESSORIES

Christine

181 Flinders Lane; tel: 03-9654 2011; Mon, Sat 10pm–5pm, Tue–Fri 10am–6pm; train: Flinders Street; tram: 75; map p.121 D3

Christine Barro scours for fashionable accessories such as scarves, belts and brooches from Australia and overseas, including fashionable Paris. You can easily find

Below: the newly refurbished David Jones.

Left: the striking roof at Melbourne Central.

Collins Place
45 Collins Street; tel: 03-9655 3600; www.collinsplace. au; Mon–Thur 9am–6pm, Fri 9am–7pm, Sat 9am–5pm, Sun 10am–5pm; tram: 72, 109, 112; map p.121 E2
This shopping arcade located at the posh 'Paris End' of Collins Street has more than 40 stores, including swanky brands like Giorgio Armani and Salvatore Ferragamo.

Collins two3four
234 Collins Street; tel: 03-9650 4373; www.collins234.com.au; trading hours vary depending on individual stores; tram: 72, 109, 112; map p.121 D3
This complex's highlights include Dymocks bookstore and designer boutiques like Saba and Lisa Barron, one of Melbourne's most respected designers, whose fans include supermodels Linda Evangelista and Naomi Campbell.

Melbourne Central
Corner of La Trobe and Swanston Streets; 03-9922 1100; www.melbournecentral.com.

of them made in Victoria or sourced from other parts of Australia.

e.g.etal Flinders Lane
Basement, 167 Flinders Lane; tel: 03-9639 5111; www.egetal. com.au; Mon–Thur 10am–6pm, Fri 10am–7pm, Sat 10am–5pm; train: Flinders Street, tram: 75; map p.121 D3
e.g.etal is a unique gallery that supports and advocates Australia's contemporary jewellery design industry. Currently it represents over 50 Australian and New Zealand jewellery artists and designers. The collection includes original and limited edition pieces – including stunning diamond engagement rings, necklaces, rings, cufflinks, earrings, bracelets and brooches.

PHOTOGRAPHY
MI Gallery
Shop 4, 239 Flinders Lane (enter via Scott Alley); tel: 03-9663 2858; www.mattirwin.com; Mon–Fri, 11am–6pm, Sat 11am–5pm, Sun noon–4pm: train: Flinders Street; map p.121 D3
Matt Irwin loves taking photographs of Melbourne and other exciting cities around the world. You might just end up buying photos of Melbourne's laneways here!

SHOPPING ARCADES
Australia on Collins
260 Collins Street; tel: 03-9650 4355; www.thakral.com.au; trading hours vary depending on individual stores; tram: 72, 109, 112; map p.121 D3
Australia on Collins has more than 60 stores, many featuring imported fashion and local stalwarts such as Country Road and David Lawrence. Top crafts retailer Lincraft is also located here.

The Block Arcade
282 Collins Street; tel: 03-9654 5255; www.theblockarcade. com.au; trading hours vary depending on individual stores; tram: 109, 112; map p.121 C3
This grand and gorgeous arcade between Collins and Little Collins Streets houses exclusive jewellery retailers, leather goods, lingerie, giftware and also the Hopetoun Tea Rooms. The unique history of this well-restored 19th-century building is under the protection of the National Trust.

Shopping tours have become one of the city's biggest tourist draw cards: they usually include lunch and can take in Melbourne's famous factory outlets and seconds shops. Or you can choose a tour that will lead you to those harder-to-find local designers who are often hidden in Melbourne's labyrinth of laneways. Check out the **Hidden Secrets Tours** (tel: 03-9329 9665; www.hiddensecretstours.com) – a Lanes and Arcades Tour that leads you to more than 50 local designers and speciality shops.

au; trading hours vary depending on individual stores; train: Melbourne Central; tram: 3, 5, 16, 19; map p.121 C2

This complex offers shopping, eating and entertaining (Hoyts Cinema is located here too) options. There are 300 stores to visit, including Borders, and lots of food outlets.

SEE ALSO LITERATURE, P.71

Melbourne's GPO

Corner of Bourke and Elizabeth Streets; tel: 03-9663 0066; www.melbournesgpo.com; Mon–Thur 10am–6pm, Fri 10am–8pm, Sat 10am–6pm, Sun 11am–5pm; tram: 96; map p.121 C2

This stunning historic building is home to a large variety of local designers such as Akira, Lisa Ho, Leona Edmiston, Metalicus, Wayne Cooper and others. There are also famous brands from Europe like Camper and Jigsaw

Royal Arcade

335 Bourke Street Mall; tel: 03-9670 7777; www.royalarcade.com.au; trading hours vary depending on individual stores; tram: 96; map p.121 C2

This is the city's oldest shopping arcade, with its Renaissance Revival style architecture dating from 1869. It is considered a hub between Bourke Street Mall, Little Collins Street and Elizabeth Street. One of the highlights here is the 1892 Gaunt's Clock – flanked by two statues of the mythical figures of Gog and Magog. Tenants include Thomas Jewellers, Koko Black (fabulous chocolate drinks and desserts) and many others.

Right: vintage finds galore at the Chapel Street Bazaar.

Spencer Street Fashion Station (formerly DFO)

201 Spencer Street, Docklands; tel: 03-8689 7555; www.spencerst.com.au; daily 10am–6pm, Friday until 9pm; train: Southern Cross; tram: 75, 86, 95; map p.120 B3

This sprawling mall adjacent to Southern Cross Station has about 120 mainstream brands. You will find clothing, shoes, bags and homeware stores at great prices.

VINTAGE
Chapel Street Bazaar

217 Chapel Street, Prahran; 03-9529 1727; daily 10am–6pm; tram: 78; map p.119 E1

This massive shop space has been around for almost two decades. It brims with stuff from yesteryear – at least the last 80 to 90 years. It is one of those places where you can snap up your favourite smurf, old camera, retro telephone, vintage movie posters, bird cages and even that old Lady Di and Prince Charles salt

and pepper shaker that you've always wanted. Foodies can head to the aisle crammed with old-fashioned kitchenware. There are also vintage dresses, suits and ties to comb through. Fancy making your own outfit? There is a section devoted to vintage sewing patterns and fabrics.

RetroStar

First floor, Nicholas Building, 37 Swanston Street (corner of Flinders Lane); tel: 03-9663 1223; www.retrostar.com.au; Mon–Thur and Sat 10am–6pm, Fri 10am–8pm, Sun 11.30am–6pm; map p.121 D3

This is the largest vintage emporium in the country, offering over 10,000 items of clothing and accessories from the 1940s to the 1980s. Find classy vintage dresses, minis with psychedelic prints, 70s flares, and many others here. Also features RetroStar Rockstar, which is dedicated to music and street wear.

Sports

To say that Melbourne is sport-obsessed is something of an understatement. This is the town that invented Australian Rules football, that hosts the country's favourite horse race and any number of international sporting events, the place where watching, playing or betting on sport is a major part of everyday life. Woe betide those who publicly profess to have no interest in sports – they are treated with a mixture of disbelief and disdain by the sports-mad majority. But this enthusiasm for sports is infectious, so don't be surprised if you find yourself asking how the Aussie Rules game is played.

SPECTATOR SPORTS

AUSTRALIAN FOOTBALL LEAGUE (AFL)

Australian Rules football – a mixture of rugby, soccer and Gaelic football – is at its best in Melbourne. Matches are held every Saturday, some Friday nights and Sundays. The AFL season starts in March each year and lasts for 22 rounds. Thereafter, the top eight teams compete in the four-week AFL Finals Series. The **Grand Final** pits the two top teams at the Melbourne Cricket Ground (MCG) (see p.102) on the last Saturday in September,

Above: watching footy in Federation Square.

before more than 100,000 fanatical supporters. Local teams include Collingwood, Geelong and Hawthorn.

Melbourne goes footy crazy during the finals – club colours are seen everywhere, pubs show televised matches on big screens, finals barbecues are popular, and there's even a street parade in central Melbourne on the Friday before the Grand Final. Unfortunately, tickets for all finals matches are extremely hard to come by. See: www.afl.com.au.

CRICKET

December to February is the season for international cricket, when matches are played at the Melbourne Cricket Ground. The **Boxing Day Test** forms the year's high-light and kicks off the season. If you're not up to the long day of Test cricket, the short and sweet Twenty20 matches only take about three hours. For more information and to buy tickets, go to the **Cricket Australia** website (www.cricket.com.au).

Sports betting is popular in Australia, and Melbourne is no exception. Popular betting agencies include Tab (www. tab.com.au), Sportingbet (www. sportingbet.com.au), BetSports (www.betsports.com.au), Sportsbet (www.sportsbet.com. au) and Betfair (www.betfair. com.au). Betting online is fairly easy, and most agencies cover a large range of sports.

and the national league was set up in 2005. The game grew further in popularity after the national team's success at the 2006 World Cup. The national league is run by **Football Federation Australia** (www.footballaustralia. com.au) and is officially known as the Hyundai A-League (www.a-league. com.au). The season starts in August and ends in February. There are a total of 11 teams in the league, and Melbourne has two in it – **Melbourne Heart** (www. melbourneheartfc.com.au) and **Melbourne Victory** (www. melbournevictory.com.au).

TENNIS

The **Australian Open** (www. australianopen.com) is one of the most popular events in the sporting calendar. The Grand Slam tournament for the Asia-Pacific region is held during the second

FORMULA ONE GRAND PRIX

March marks the time for the **Australian Formula One Grand Prix** (www. grandprix.com.au), at Albert Park. It's not just on the track that you can hear the buzz – areas like Lygon Street in Carlton come alive, thanks to the huge concentration of Ferrari fans there.

SEE ALSO PARKS AND GARDENS, P.86

HORSE RACING

Races are held all year, on the metropolitan courses at Flemington, Caulfield, Moonee Valley and Sandown. To find out what races are taking place, log on to www.racingvictoria. net.au. The biggest event on the racing calendar is, undoubtedly, the **Melbourne Cup** (www.melbournecup.com). The internationally famous racing event is held in spring, on the first Tuesday in November, at Flemington, which is northwest of the city centre.

The **Spring Racing Carnival** is a massive day in the city; thousands of people put on their smartest outfits, including hats, of course, and head to the racecourse for a day of fun – and hopefully some winnings too. It's no wonder that it's called the 'Race That Stops a Nation'.

Other popular Spring Carnival events are **Oaks Day** and **Derby Day** at Flemington (www.vrc.net. au), the **Caulfield Cup** at Caulfield Racecourse (www.melbourneracingclub.net. au) and the **Cox Plate** at Moonee Valley Racecourse (www.mvrc.net.au).

SEE ALSO FESTIVALS AND EVENTS, P.49

Flemington Racecourse
448 Epsom Road, Flemington; tel: 1300 727 575; www.flemington.com.au
Melbourne's home of horse racing and host of the Spring Racing Carnival.

SOCCER

This sport has grown in popularity in recent years,

half of January each year at Melbourne Park. The world's best slog it out in often sweltering conditions (40°C/104°F is not unusual), and the crowd is vociferous in its support of local contenders and visiting favourites.

MAJOR VENUES
Etihad Stadium
740 Bourke Street, Docklands; tel: 03-8625 7700; www.etihadstadium.com.au; map p.120 A3
Just minutes from the CBD, this stadium is the only football stadium in the Southern Hemisphere with a fully retractable roof. It opened in 2000 and has let in more than 19 million people since.

Melbourne Cricket Ground (MCG)
Brunton Avenue, Richmond; tel: 03-9657 8888; www.mcg.org.au; map p.117 D1
This world-famous sporting ground and Australian

shrine is close to the heart of any self-respecting sports fan. Home to the 1956 Olympics, the 'G hosts many major sporting events, including regular matches of Australian Rules football and international cricket. Tours available.

Melbourne and Olympic Parks
Batman Avenue, Melbourne; tel: 03-9286 1600; www.mopt.com.au; map p.117 C1
Multiple venues host tennis, rugby, basketball and netball. Consists of Rod Laver Arena, Hisense Arena, AAMI Park and Olympic Park Stadium.

PARTICIPANT SPORTS

GOLF

Melbourne harbours some of Australia's top courses in the famed 'sandbelt' region in the southeastern suburbs. All 'sandbelt' clubs are private, although golf tour operators such

Whether you're taking part in sports or just watching from the sidelines, remember to protect yourself against the sun, especially during the warmer months. Use sunblock and wear clothing that covers most of your body. Wear a wide hat and try to stay in the shade as much as possible.

as **Gimme Golf** (www.gimmegolf.com.au) can organise access to exclusive courses, provided players meet the clubs' strict requirements. Failing that, Melbourne has some of the nation's best public links. The **Victorian Golf Association** website (www.golfvic.org.au) has a comprehensive listing of clubs in the state.

Huntingdale
Windsor Avenue, South Oakleigh; tel: 03-9579 4622

Metropolitan
Golf Road, South Oakleigh; tel: 03-9579 3122

Below: match days at the famous MCG are always packed out.

Above: a skier takes a break on Mount Buller.

Royal Melbourne
Cheltenham Road, Black Rock;
tel: 03-9598 6755

Yarra Bend
Yarra Bend Road, Fairfield; tel:
03-9481 3729

WATERSPORTS

Port Phillip Bay offers
excellent sailing condi-
tions, and yacht clubs
are plentiful. Swimmers
should head to the
Melbourne Sports and
Aquatic Centre (MSAC),
the largest integrated
sports complex of its
type in Australia, on the
edge of Albert Park Lake.
Melbourne's Yarra River
is great for canoeing and
kayaking.

**Fairfield Park
Boathouse**
Fairfield Park Drive, Fairfield;
tel: 03-9486 1501; www.fair
fieldboathouse.com
Located on the Yarra
River. Canoes, kayaks and
rowing skiffs for hire.

**Melbourne
City Baths**
420 Swanston Street, Mel-
bourne; tel: 03-9663 5888

**Repeat Performance
Sailboards**
87 Ormond Road, Elwood; tel:
03-9525 6475
Equipment hire.

**Melbourne Sports and
Aquatic Centre**
Aughtie Drive, Albert Park;
tel: 03-9926 1555; www.msac.
com.au
For those who love being
in the water.

**Sandringham Harbour
Headquarters**
81 Beach Road, Sandringham;
tel: 03-9598 2867
Learn windsurfing or kite
boarding here.
    The abundance of wind
on Port Phillip Bay
makes Melbourne a popu-
lar location for windsurfing and kite boarding.
Elwood and St Kilda are
also popular spots.

SNOW SPORTS

During a good season,
an easy place to access
the snow from Melbourne
is **Lake Mountain** (www.
lakemountainresort.com.au), a
popular cross-country ski
resort. There are also several toboggan runs here.
    Further afield, **Mount
Buller** (www.mtbuller.com.
au), **Mount Hotham** (www.
mthotham.com.au) and **Falls
Creek** (www.fallscreek.com.
au) are major downhill ski
resorts with several runs.
    The Victorian Snow
Report has up-to-date
information on snow, road
and weather conditions
(www.vicsnowreport.com.au).

Tickets for many sporting
events are available from the
two main ticketing agencies,
Ticketek (www.ticketek.com.
au) and TicketMaster (www.
ticketmaster.com.au). The
more popular events sell out
fast, so book early to avoid
disappointment.

Theatre and Dance

Melbourne is noted for its high-quality performances of comedy, theatre and dance. There are always theatre productions at the city's major arts venue, the Arts Centre. Other major commercial theatres include the grand Princess Theatre, Her Majesty's Theatre and the spectacularly refurbished Regent Theatre. The best listings for Melbourne's lively performing arts scene can be found in the Entertainment Guide (EG) in every Friday issue of *The Age* newspaper or the free weekly street press: *Inpress* and *Beat*. For theatre, the quickest way to find out what's on is to log on to Theatre Alive (www.theatrealive.com.au).

THEATRE

The major theatre company in Melbourne is the **Melbourne Theatre Company** (www.mtc.com.au). Its productions appear at the MTC Theatre at Southbank Boulevard and the Arts Centre at nearby St Kilda Road.

The city's second theatre company is the **Malthouse Theatre** (www.malthouse theatre.com.au), based at the CUB Malthouse on Sturt Street in Southbank.

Theatre events in Melbourne – including musicals – are held at the Arts Centre, Her Majesty's Theatre and the Princess, Regent and Comedy theatres.

Below: the CUB Malthouse.

Those looking for more adventurous works can check out **fortyfivedownstairs** (www.fortyfivedownstairs. com) on Flinders Lane, **Red Stitch Actors' Theatre** (www.redstitch.net) in St Kilda, **La Mama** (www.lamama.com. au) in Carlton and **Theatreworks** (www.theatreworks. au) in St Kilda.

VENUES

The Arts Centre

100 St Kilda Road; tel: 03-9281 8000; www.theartscentre.net. au; train: Flinders Street; map p.121 D4

Australia's and the world's leading companies perform here, including the Royal Shakespeare Company and the Sydney Dance Company.

Comedy Theatre

240 Exhibition Street; tel: 03-9299 4950; www.marriner theatres.com.au; train: Parliament; map p.121 D1

Built on the original location of the Hippodrome, famous names that have graced this theatre include Rex Harrison and Vincent Price.

Forum Theatre

Corner of Russell and Flinders Streets; tel: 03-9299 9860; www.marrinertheatres.com. au; train: Flinders Street; map p.121 D3

Formerly the Old State Theatre, this is one of the most beautiful theatres in Melbourne, and plays host to theatre performances and concerts.

Her Majesty's Theatre

219 Exhibition Street; tel: 03-8643 3300; www.hmt.com. au; train: Parliament; map p.121 D2

Musicals, opera and ballet are all performed in this historic theatre. The theatre is currently owned by Mike Walsh OBE, a multi-award-winning television personality, who bought it in November 1999, then commenced on major renovations to restore it.

MTC Theatre

140 Southbank Boulevard; tel: 03-8688 0800; www.mtc.com. au; train: Flinders Street; map p.116 B2

You won't miss this build-

Left: queuing for a show at Her Majesty's Theatre.

formance in contemporary dance, and gives performances in its studios and elsewhere around the city.

OPERA

The Victoria State Opera merged with the Sydney-based Australian Opera in the 1990s to form **Opera Australia** (www.opera-australia.org.au). Most performances are now in Sydney, but there are regular seasons in Melbourne's Arts Centre. The local torch is now carried by **Victorian Opera** (www.victorianopera.com.au), which is rapidly establishing a name for itself with backing from the State Government, and performing throughout Victoria, as well as at various venues in the city.

TICKETS

Tickets for theatre, sport, music and other events are often sold through agencies. The two main ticket agencies are **Ticketek** (tel: 132 849; www.ticketek.com.au) and **Ticketmaster** (Theatre and Arts tel: 1300-723 038; Arts Centre tel: 1300-136 166; www.ticketmaster.com.au).

The Melbourne International Comedy Festival is a massive annual event, first launched in 1987 by Barry Humphries and Peter Cook. It is one of the three largest comedy festivals in the world, alongside Edinburgh Festival Fringe and Montreal's Just for Laughs Festival. This festival takes place in March/April, with roadshows and other related events happening throughout the year. www.comedyfestival.com.au. See also Nightlife, p.84.

ing, with its distinctive white piping. It houses the Summer Theatre, a 500-seat venue, and the 150-seat Lawler Studio. Productions that have taken place here include *Richard III* and *All about My Mother*.

Princess Theatre
163 Spring Street; tel: 03-9299 9800; www.marrinertheatres.com.au; train: Parliament; map p.121 D1
A historic venue where big-budget productions such as *Phantom of the Opera* and *Cats* are staged. It was built in 1886

and is considered by many as the most spectacular landmark in Melbourne.

Regent Theatre
191 Collins Street; tel: 03-9299 9800; www.marrinertheatres.com.au; train: Flinders Street; map p.121 D3
After being through numerous reincarnations, the lavishly restored Regent Theatre reopened in 1996, with Andrew Lloyd Webber's *Sunset Boulevard*. The theatre, which once showed silent films, has since hosted shows such as *Wicked* and *Singin' in the Rain*.

DANCE
The national company, the **Australian Ballet** (www.australianballet.com.au), is based in Melbourne and runs regular seasons at the Arts Centre.

Chunky Move (www.chunkymove.com) has gained an international reputation for its programme of genre-defying dance productions.

Dancehouse (www.dancehouse.com.au) is a centre for research, training and per-

Below: performing *Moonlight* at the MTC Theatre.

Transport

The vast majority of visitors to Victoria arrive by air. There are also various rail (www.vline.com.au) and bus (www.greyhound.com.au) links from within the country, if you are visiting domestically and want to take the more scenic route during your travels. And, of course, the option of driving interstate is also possible. A car will also be of considerable use if you wish to get out into the Dandenong Ranges and, of course, the Great Ocean Road. But once in Melbourne's straightforward city centre, there are many ways to get around conveniently, such as trains, buses and trams, including a free one.

GETTING THERE

Melbourne Airport (tel: 03-9297 1600; www.melbourneairport.com.au) is 22km (14 miles) northwest of the city centre, and **Avalon Airport** (tel: 1800 282 566; www.avalonairport.com.au) sits 55km (34 miles) southwest of the city centre.

Shuttle bus services are available at both airports – **Skybus** (tel: 03-9335 2811; www.skybus.com.au; adult A$16 one way, A$26 return) from Melbourne Airport and **Sita Coaches** (tel: 03-9689 7999; www.sitacoaches.com.au/avalon; A$20 one way, A$36 return) from Avalon Airport. Both go to Southern Cross Station or city hotels. Bookings are essential.

GETTING AROUND

PUBLIC TRANSPORT

Melbourne's public transport system is run by **Metlink** (tel: 131 638; www.metlinkmelbourne.com.au) and comprises trams, buses and trains. Visit the **Met-Shop** (Mon–Fri 8.30am–5.30pm, Sat 9am–1pm) on the ground floor of the Melbourne Town Hall for information and tickets.

Metcards (tickets) offer unlimited travel over various periods (for example two hours, one day, one week) and throughout various zones (zone 1 is enough for most visitors' purposes). They can be used on metropolitan trams, buses and trains (excluding airport services).

It's cheaper to purchase a Metcard in advance; these are available from newsstands and convenience stores displaying the blue Metcard sign, train stations, the MetShop, the Melbourne Visitor Centre at Federation Square or online.

Get two-hour and one-day tickets from machines on board trams, from bus drivers and from machines or ticket booths at railway stations. If using a machine, you must pay with coins. You must validate the Metcard

Below: the yellow taxis are easy to spot in the city centre.

Left: the city's tram network is straightforward and efficient.

DRIVING

Traffic drives on the left in Australia. Vic Roads (www.vicroads.vic.gov.au) provides information about road rules and licensing.

There is a 0.05 percent blood alcohol limit for drivers, and random breath tests are carried out by the police. Random drug tests are also done.

There are multi-storey car parks in the CBD, as well as street parking. In suburban areas, street parking can be free or metered.

To rent a car for excursions into regional Victoria, you must be over 25 and possess a full licence in your country of origin. You will need a copy of the licence in English or an International Driving Permit, your passport and a credit card to which a pre-authorised security bond can be charged. Drivers between 18 and 25 may be able to hire a vehicle if they pay a surcharge.

Car rental firms with offices in central Melbourne and desks at the airports include **Avis** (tel: 136 333; www.avis.com.au), **Budget** (tel: 1300 362 848; www.budget.com.au), **Europcar** (tel: 1300 131 390; www.europcar.com.au) and **Thrifty** (tel: 1300 367 227; www.thrifty.com.au).

in the machine on board the bus or tram, or at the train station.

Melbourne is currently moving from Metcards to a new smartcard ticketing system called **myki**. Visitors are recommended to continue buying Metcards at this time.

FREE CITY TRANSPORT

The free City Circle tram operates around the outer edge of the CBD. Old 'W'-class trams painted brown, they stop close to major tourist attractions including Docklands, Federation Square and the Melbourne Museum.

There's also the Melbourne City Tourist Shuttle bus that goes on a different route. Sights include the arts precinct, Chinatown and Queen Victoria market.

TAXIS

You can hail one of Melbourne's yellow taxis in the street if its rooftop light is on. Taxi ranks can be found at major hotels

Above: Melbourne's roads are clearly signposted.

or busy locations such as train stations. There are surcharges for phone bookings, and for trips between midnight and 5am, departing from the airport taxi rank and using toll roads.

The major companies are **Silver Top Taxis** (tel: 131 008; www.silvertop.com.au) and **13 CABS** (aka Black Cabs; tel: 132 227; www.yellowcabs.com.au).

Travelling long distances isn't necessarily good for the environment, so why not 'offset' the carbon produced by your journey? While in Australia, log on to www.carbonoffsetguide.com.au and see how you can participate in the programme.

Vineyards

Barely an hour's drive from the city centre brings you to stunning wineries, some with very rich histories. Yarra Valley is one of the most picturesque wine regions in Australia, and a significant wine and tourism destination. The area has a rich 150-year history in winemaking, and in the past 15 years or so the spotlight has been shining on its various award-winning estates. The Mornington Peninsula, meanwhile, has 50 cellar doors – the gentle maritime climate puts its individual stamp on the boutique wines produced. Make a day trip to the winery of your choice or spend the night to soak up the full atmosphere.

YARRA VALLEY

Balgownie Estate Vineyard Resort & Spa

Melba Highway and Gulf Road, Yarra Glen; tel: 03-5962 2600; www.balgownieestate.com.au; Cellar Door daily 10am–5pm, Restaurant daily 7.30–10.30am, noon–3pm, dinner from 6pm
Besides a Cellar Door, there is even a wine museum here. The restaurant uses local produce to create dishes influenced by French, Italian and Asian cuisines. The luxurious resort accommodation affords magnificent views of the Yarra Valley from private balconies.
SEE ALSO HOTELS, P.66

De Bortoli Wines

58 Pinnacle Lane, Dixons Creek; tel: 03-5965 2271; www.debortoli.com.au; Cellar Door and Cheese Room daily 10am–5pm
A long avenue lined with shady Manchurian Pear trees leads you to De Bortoli. Established in 1928, this is a third-generation family wine estate. Started by Vittorio and Giuseppina

Above: a tasting session at Domaine Chandon.

De Bortoli who emigrated from northern Italy, the business continues to flourish in the 21st century. The winery is most famous for its signature dessert wine, Noble One Botrytis Semillon. Besides the Cellar Door, there is also a Cheese Room displaying all kinds of quality cheeses and a restaurant serving superb Italian-style dishes.
SEE ALSO RESTAURANTS, P.95

Domaine Chandon

727 Maroondah Highway, Coldstream; tel: 03-9738 9200; www.domainechandon.com.au; daily 10.30am–4.30pm, light lunches available 11am–4pm (closed on Christmas Day)
Established in 1986 by Moët & Chandon, Domaine Chandon's wines have been lauded for their style and quality, both in Australia and internationally. 'Green Point', as it is also known, has been inducted into the Victorian Tourism Hall of Fame, having won the Winery Tourism category three times.

Millers Dixons Creek Estate

1620 Melba Highway, Dixons Creek; tel: 03-5965 2396; www.graememillerwines.com.au; Cellar Door daily 10am–5pm
Winemaker Graeme Miller was one of the pioneers during the rebirth of the Yarra Valley as a wine region, in the 1960s and 1970s. Get a view of a working winery or simply take in the history of the Yarra Valley wine industry, which is on display here.

Left: the Yarra Valley is laced with vineyards.

the likes of Tom Jones, Ronan Keating and Diana Krall.

MORNINGTON PENINSULA
Dromana Estate Café & Cellar Door
555 Old Moorooduc Road, Tuerong; tel: 03-5974 1155; www.dromanaestate.com.au; Cellar Door noon–4pm Wed–Sun, Café 11am–5pm Wed–Sun
Housed in the historic 100-year-old Tuerong park homestead, Dromana Estate has been producing award-winning cool-climate Pinot Noir and Chardonnay for over 10 years now. Dine alfresco in the English gardens or pick up a bargain at the Cellar Door.

Lindenderry at Red Hill
142 Arthurs Seat Road, Red Hill; tel: 03-5989 2933; www.lancemore.com.au; Sat–Sun 11am–5pm
The wood-fired pizzas are a must-try, as are the award-winning, single-vineyard wines. Premium Sparkling Rosé, Pinot Noir, Chardonnay, Pinot Gris, Merlot, Shiraz and Cabernet are available for tasting at the Cellar Door.

Ocean Eight Vineyard & Winery
271 Tucks Road, Shoreham; tel: 03-5989 5371; www.oceaneight.com; tastings between noon and 4pm, Sat/Sun on the first weekend of each month, open on public holidays
Produces quality Pinot Noir, Chardonnay and Pinot Gris, and was given five stars in the *Halliday Wine Guide* 2011.

The Macedon Ranges wine region is another area worth visiting, with its cool to cold climate contributing to wine that is limited in quantity and exceptionally high in quality. It is located about an hour from Melbourne too. www.macedonrangeswine.com.au

Oakridge Wines
864 Maroondah Highway, Coldstream; tel: 03-9739 1920; www.oakridgewines.com.au; Cellar Door daily 10am–5pm (closed on Christmas Day)
Produces fine examples of cool-climate wine styles, and its Chardonnay has won various trophies. Also produces the acclaimed 864 range of wines, which is named after its address. The café serves light lunches, and valley views are spectacular here.

Rochford Wines
Corner of Maroondah Highway and Hill Road, Coldstream; tel: 03-5962 2119; www.rochfordwines.com.au; Cellar Door and Café daily 10am–5pm, restaurant daily noon–3pm
Join a private tasting or choose to weave through renowned Australian artworks in the elevated Pinot Gallery. Climb up to the Viewing Tower and enjoy the 360-degree view. Buy some of its estate-made kumquat jam at the Produce Store or share a bottle of its award-winning Macedon Ranges Pinot Noir in the restaurant. Rochford Wines also organises exciting concerts and events and has hosted

Below: checking the barrels.

Wildlife

Australia is known for a range of unique animals such as kangaroos, koalas, echidnas, platypus and the Tasmanian devil. There are plenty of opportunities to get up close with these and other animals in Melbourne. Attractions like Melbourne Zoo and Melbourne Aquarium are easily accessible from the city, but there are also places somewhat further out, such as Healesville Sanctuary and Phillip Island, that are certainly worth the trek. There are many wildlife conservation efforts in Australia, and Melbourne is doing its part.

HEALESVILLE SANCTUARY

Badger Creek Road, Healesville; tel: 03-5957 2800; www.zoo.org.au/HealesvilleSanctuary; daily 9am–5pm; charge; train: Lilydale, then bus 685 or 686 to Healesville

This is the place to see the best of Australian wildlife. Australian native animals that call Healesville home include the dingo, koala, platypus and Tasmanian devil.

Experience what it is like to really be close to the animals, with experiences such as Keeper for a Morning and Vet Assistant for a Morning. Adults can make a day out of it and join the Wine and Wildlife tour. Most experiences incur extra charges, check website for details.
SEE ALSO CHILDREN, P.40

LA TROBE WILDLIFE SANCTUARY

Melbourne (Bundoora) campus of La Trobe University, Main Drive, Bundoora; tel: 03-9479 1206; www.latrobe.edu.au/wildlife; Sun–Fri 10am–3pm; charge; tram: 86

Set up in 1967 as a project for the restoration and management of indigenous flora and fauna, this sanctuary has grown into an ideal destination for wildlife fans. Birdwatching is possible here, and those who are into reptiles can check out the lizard lounges. The sanctuary is home to around 19 species of reptiles, mostly from the Scinicidae family. Aussie animals can be seen here too, such as the kangaroo, echidna and platypus.

MELBOURNE AQUARIUM

Corner of King and Flinders Streets, Melbourne; tel: 03-9923 5999; www.melbourneaquarium.com.au; daily 9.30am–6pm, 1–26 Jan 9.30am–9pm (last admission one hour before closing); charge; train: Flinders Street or Southern Cross

There are a few worlds to discover at the aquarium. Sharks Alive has a view

Above: see dingoes at Healesville Sanctuary.

that makes you feel like you are underwater with these animals. Those brave enough can dive in and swim with the sharks too (additional charges apply). Other worlds to experience here are Antarctica, River to Reef and Weird & Wonderful.
SEE ALSO CHILDREN, P.40

MELBOURNE ZOO

Elliott Avenue, Parkville; tel: 03-9285 9300; www.zoo.org.au/MelbourneZoo; daily 9am–5pm; charge; train: Royal Park

Get acquainted with various animals from Australia and beyond. Unique experiences include Elephant Encounters, Tiger Territory and Reptile House. Summer programme includes Zoo Twilights, with music at the Melbourne Zoo. If you have never been near a kangaroo or koala before, this is your chance–you can pat a koala, feed a tree kangaroo and have your photo taken with them too. Additional charges apply, check website for details.

SEE ALSO CHILDREN, P.41

PHILLIP ISLAND NATURE PARKS

1019 Ventnor Road, Summerlands; tel: 03-5951 2830; www. penguins.org.au; 10am, closing times vary; charge

The Penguin Parade is the main attraction here, and that certainly makes it worth the 90-minute drive from the city. Also worth a look is the Koala Conservation Centre, where visitors can experience koalas in their natural habitat as well as enjoy bush walking tracks. Most major tour companies run tours to the island daily.

PHILLIP ISLAND WILDLIFE PARK

2115 Phillip Island Road, Cowes; tel: 03-5952 2038; www.piwildlifepark.com.au; daily 10am, closing times vary throughout the year; charge

There are more than 100 different species of Australian animals here, over 24 hectares (60 acres) of land. You will find the likes of kangaroos and wallabies roaming the grounds, and you can even pat and

Left: look out for lions at Werribee Open Range Zoo.

hand-feed them. You will be able to see Koalas eye to eye here, as viewing takes place on a raised boardwalk. Bird-watchers will be thrilled too, with species such as the flightless emu, parrots, cockatoos and various species of owls found here.

WERRIBEE OPEN RANGE ZOO

K Road, Werribee; tel: 03-9731 9600; www.zoo.org.au/Werri beeOpenRangeZoo; daily 9am–5pm; charge; train: Werribee

Get out of the city and get up close with some unique wildlife. You would be forgiven for thinking that you are actually on safari somewhere in Africa. The zoo is spread over 225 hectares (563 acres) and animals that live here include the zebra, lion, rhino, giraffe and meerkat. You can also opt to go on an open vehicle adventure (additional charges apply), where you will travel across the zoo's open plains, surrounded by wildlife.

Below: look out for penguin-safety signs at Phillip Island Wildlife Park.

Please
CHECK UNDER YOUR CAR
Before driving away

Atlas

The following streetplan of Melbourne makes it easy to find the attractions listed in the A–Z section. A selective index to streets and sights will help you find other locations throughout the city

Map Legend

≡≡≡	Motorway	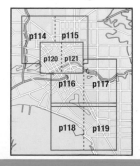 Metlink station	
	Dual carriageway	Bus station	
	Main road	Post office	
	Minor road	Viewpoint	
	Pedestrian road	Airport	
	Footpath	Tourist information	
	Railway	Sight of interest	
	Pedestrian area	Cathedral/church	
	Notable building	Museum/gallery	
	Park	Theatre/concert hall	
	Hotel	Synagogue	
	Urban area	Statue/monument	
	Non urban area	Hospital	
	Cemetery		

p114 | p115

p120 | p121

p116 | p117

p118 | p119

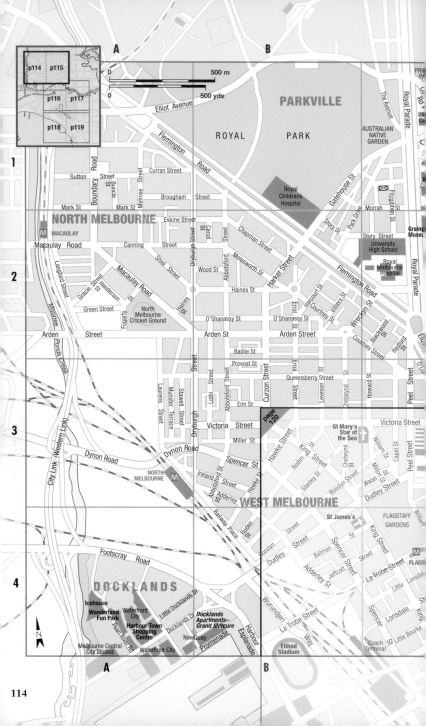

0   500 m

0   500 yds

PARKVILLE

ROYAL   PARK

Elliot Avenue

AUSTRALIAN NATIVE GARDEN

The Avenue

Royal Parade

PRIN PA

Co

1

Flemington Road

Road

Sutton

Boundary

Street

Bundle St

Melrose Street

Curran Street

Brougham Street

Street

Mark St

Mark St

Royal Childrens Hospital

Gatehouse St

Park Drive

Story St

Morrah

Fitzgibbon St

NORTH MELBOURNE

Ⓜ MACAULAY

Eskine Street

Dryburgh Street

Curzon St

Chapman Street

Story Street

University High School

Grainger Muse

Macaulay Road

Canning Street

Street

Shiel Street

Harker Street

Molesworth St

Abbotsford

Flemington Road

Royal Melbourne Hospital

Royal Parade

2

Macaulay Road

Gracie Street

Henderson St

Langford Street

Moonee Ponds Creek

Green Street

Fogarty

Haines

St

North Melbourne Cricket Ground

Wood St

Haines St

O'Shanassy St

O'Shanassy St

Harcourt St

Courtney St

Errol

Villiers St

Wreckyn St

Courtney Street

Blackwood St

Bedford St

Arden   Street

Arden St

Arden Street

Street

Baillie St

Provost St

Errol

Peel Street

O'C

3

City Link (Western Link)

Dynon Road

Dynon Road

Street

Laurens Street

Stawell Street

Munster Terrace

Dryburgh

Loth Street

Abbotsford Street

Victoria   Street

Miller St

Elm St

Queensberry Street

Leveson

Curzon Street

Chetwynd

Street

Howard St

Page 120

Hawke Street

King Street

Roden

St Mary's Star of the Sea

Chetwynd St

William St

Victoria Street

Miller St

Capel Street

Peel Street

Spencer St

Ireland

Street

Adderley St

Abbotsford St

Hawke St

Stanley St

Rosslyn Street

Walsh St

Dudley St

WEST MELBOURNE

NORTH MELBOURNE Ⓜ

Railway Place

Roden St

St James's

FLAGSTAFF GARDENS

King Street

FLAGS

4

City Link (Western Link)

Footscray   Road

DOCKLANDS

Icehouse

Wonderland Fun Park

Waterfront City

Harbour Town Shopping Centre

Little Docklands Dr

Pearl River Rd

Docklands Dr

Melbourne Central City Studios

Waterfront City

NewQuay

Docklands Apartments– Grand Mercure

Harbour Esplanade

Promenade

Wurundjeri

Rosslyn

Dudley

Batman

Street

Adderley St

Jeffcott

Spencer Street

Street

La Trobe Street

La Trobe Street

Spencer

Little Lonsdale

Lonsdale

Jeffcott St

Way

Etihad Stadium

Coach Terminal

Little Bourke

King

N

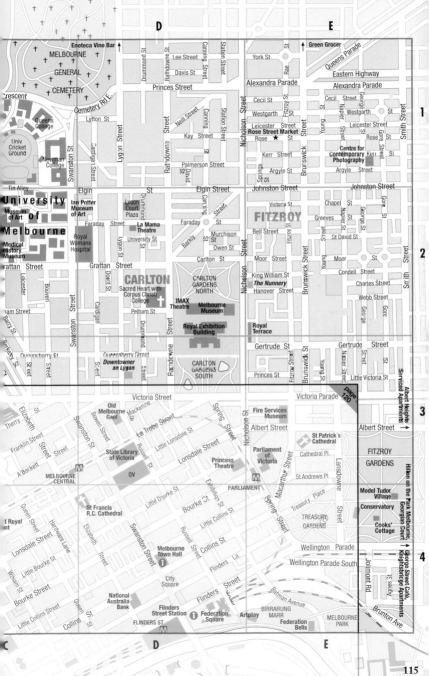

D **E**

Enoteca Vino Bar

MELBOURNE
GENERAL
CEMETERY

Green Grocer

Queens Parade

York St
Rae St

Lee Street

Davis St

Canning Street

Station Street

Rathdowne St

Drummond St

Crescent

Cemetery Rd E.

Princes Street

Alexandra Parade

Eastern Highway

Alexandra Parade

Lytton St

Nicholson Street

Cecil St
Fitzroy St
Westgarth
Rose St

Cecil Street
Westgarth
Young Street
Napier Street
George St

Leicester Street
Rose St

Smith Street

Queens
College

Cardigan Street

Lyg'n Street

Neill Street

Canning

Kay Street

St David St

Palmerson Street

Rose Street Market ★

Kerr Street

Brunswick St

Springs St

Argyle St

Centre for
Contemporary
Photography

Leicester Street
Kerr Street

Argyle Street

Gore Street

Univ
Cricket
Ground

Newman
College

Swanston St

Rathdowne

Street

David St

Elgin St

Elgin Street

Canning
Street

Johnston Street

Johnston Street

Victoria St

FITZROY

Chapel St

Gore St

University

Ian Potter
Museum
of Art

Lygon
Court
Plaza

Drummond

Faraday

Greeves St

George St

of

Museum
of Art

Faraday Street

La Mama
Theatre

Faraday

Bell Street

Fitzroy St

St David St

Napier St

Melbourne

Royal
Womans
Hospital

Lygon St

University St

Barkly St

Murchison
St
Owen St

Moor Street

Brunswick Street

Young St

Moor St

Smith Street

Medical
History
Museum

Carlton St

King William St
The Nunnery

Condell Street

Gore St

Grattan Street

Grattan Street

Dorrit St

Cardigan

CARLTON

Sacred Heart with
Corpus Christi
College

**CARLTON
GARDENS
NORTH**

Nicholson Street

Hanover Street

Charles Street

Webb Street

George St

Leicester

Bouverie

IMAX
Theatre

Melbourne
Museum

ham Street

Barry St

Queensberry St

Swanston

Drummond

Randowne

Street

Pelham St

Royal Exhibition
Building

Royal
Terrace

Gertrude St

Gertrude Street

Brunswick St

Young St

Nicholson St

Little Victoria St

Downtowner
an Lygon

Queensberry Street

**CARLTON
GARDENS
SOUTH**

Princes St

Fitzroy Street

Brunswick St

Young St

Little Victoria St

Albert Heights
Serviced Apartments

Victoria Street

Victoria Street

Victoria Parade

page 120

Albert Street →

E

Therry St

Elizabeth St

Bowen Street

Mackenzie

Old
Melbourne
Gaol

Spring Street

Fire Services
Museum

Albert Street

St Patrick's
Cathedral

**FITZROY
GARDENS**

Franklin Street

Swanston Street

La Trobe Street

Little Lonsdale Street

Nicholson St

Parliament
of
Victoria

Cathedral Pl.

A Beckett St

State Library
of Victoria

Lonsdale Street

Princess
Theatre

St Andrews Pl.

Model Tudor
Village

Hilton on the Park Melbourne,
Georgian Court

**MELBOURNE
CENTRAL**

QV

Little Bourke St

Exhibition St

PARLIAMENT

Macarthur Street

Conservatory

Queen Street

St Francis
R.C. Cathedral

Bourke St

Little Bourke St

Spring Street

Treasury Place

TREASURY
GARDENS

Cooks'
Cottage

Hardware Lane

Elizabeth Street

Little Collins St

Lonsdale Street

Swanston Street

Collins St

Wellington Parade

George Street Café,
Knightsbridge Apartments

Royal
nt

Melbourne
Town Hall

Flinders La.

Wellington Parade South

Bourke Street

Russell Street

City
Square

Flinders Street

Jolimont Rd

Selby St

Little Bourke Street

National
Australia
Bank

Flinders
Street Station

Federation
Square

Batman Avenue

BIRRARUNG
MARR

MELBOURNE
PARK

Brunton Ave

Little Collins Street

Queen St

Collins St

FLINDERS ST

Artplay

Federation
Bells

C **D** **E**

115

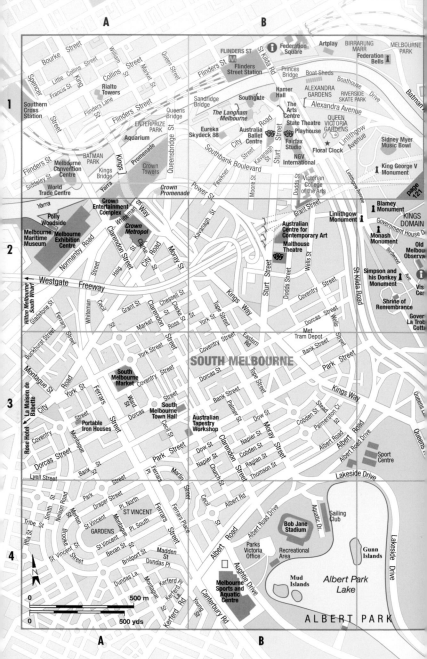

A

Bourke Street
Little Collins Street
William Street
King Street
Market Street
Queen Street
Little Collins St
Collins St
Collins Street
Francis St
Rialto Towers
Flinders Lane
Spencer Street
Flinders Street
Southern Cross Station
Queensbridge St
ENTERPRIZE PARK
Aquarium
Kings Street
Promenade
Melbourne Convention Centre
BATMAN PARK
Kings Bridge
Crown Towers
Flinders St
Sidseley St
World Trade Centre
Yarra
Crown Promenade

B

FLINDERS ST M
Flinders Street Station
St Kilda Rd
Federation Square ℹ
Artplay
BIRRARUNG MARR
MELBOURNE PARK
Federation Bells 🕴
Princes Bridge
Boat Sheds
Sandridge Bridge
Southgate
Hamer Hall
ALEXANDRA GARDENS
Boathouse
RIVERSIDE SKATE PARK
Batman Drive
The Langham Melbourne
The Arts Centre
Alexandra Avenue
City Road
Eureka Skydeck 88
Australia Ballet Centre
State Theatre
Playhouse
QUEEN VICTORIA GARDENS
Linlithgow Avenue
Southbank Boulevard
Fairfax Studio
Floral Clock ★
Sidney Myer Music Bowl
NGV International
Moore St
Sturt Street
Kavanagh St
Fawkner St
Power St
Victorian College of the Arts
Dodds St
King George V Monument 🕴
page 121

1

2

Yarra
Crown Entertainment Complex
St Way
Whiteman St
Clarke Road
Grant Street
Linlithgow Monument 🕴
Blamey Monument 🕴
KINGS DOMAIN
Polly Woodside
Crown Metropol
Clarendon Street
City Road
Moray St
Australian Centre for Contemporary Art
Government House Dr
Melbourne Maritime Museum
Melbourne Exhibition Centre
Normanby Road
Haig St
Malthouse Theatre
Sturt Street
Dodds Street
Wells Street
Monash Monument 🕴
Old Melbou Observa
Westgate Freeway
Hilton Melbourne South Wharf
Gladstone St
Ferrars St
Whiteman St
Cecil St
Grant St
Chessall St
Clarke St
Market St
Ross St
Clarendon St
York Street
Tope Street
Coventry Street
Met. Tram Depot
Wells Street
Dorcas Street
Simpson and his Donkey Monument 🕴
Shrine of Remembrance
St Kilda Road
Vis Cer ℹ
Gover La Trob Cotta

3

Buckhurst Street
Montague St
York Street
Coventry Street
SOUTH MELBOURNE
Dorcas St
Bank Street
Park Street
Kings Way
La Maison de Babette
Rose Hotel
Road
City
York St
Ferrars Street
South Melbourne Market
Ward St
Dorcas
South Melbourne Town Hall
Coventry Street
Australian Tapestry Workshop
Bank Street
Palmer St
Dow St
Cobden St
Stead St
Palmerston St
Queens Rd
Portable Iron Houses
Montague Street
Street
Cecil St
Napier St
Moray Street
Albert Road
Sport Centre
Coventry
Bank St
Dow St
Napier St
Clarendon Street
Cobden St
Church St
Raglan St
Thomson St
Albert Road Drive
Lakeside Drive
Dorcas Street
Lyell Street
Park Street
Martin St
Ferrars Pl

4

Smith St
Nelson Road
Park Street
Draper Street
Pl. North
ST VINCENT GARDENS
Ferrars Street
Ferrars Place
Cecil St
Albert Rd
Sailing Club
Tribe St
Iffla St
Merton St
Brooke St
Montague St
St Vincent
Pl. South
St Vincent Street
Bevan St
Bridport St
Madden St
Dundas Pl.
Dundas La.
Montague
Kerferd Pl
Kerferd La.
Kerferd Rd
Young St
Canterbury Rd
Melbourne Sports and Aquatic Centre
Aughtie Drive
Albert Road Drive
Parks Victoria Office
Bob Jane Stadium
Recreational Area
Aquatic Dr.
Mud Islands
Gunn Islands
Albert Park Lake
Lakeside Drive
ALBERT PARK

N

0   500 m
0   500 yds

A

B

116

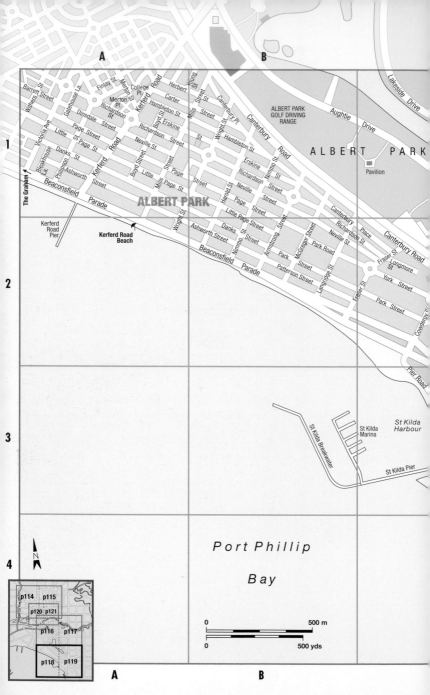

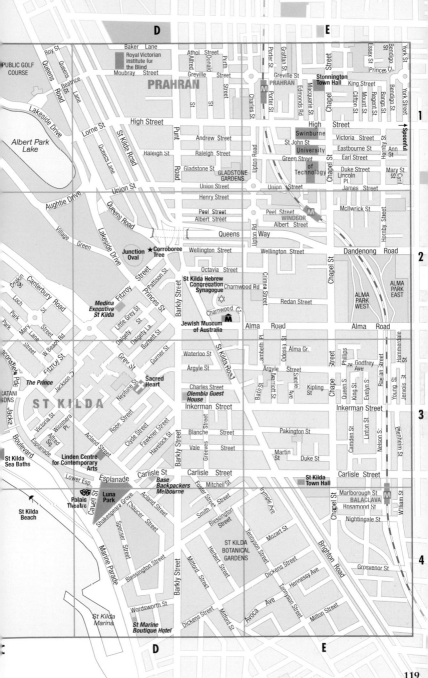

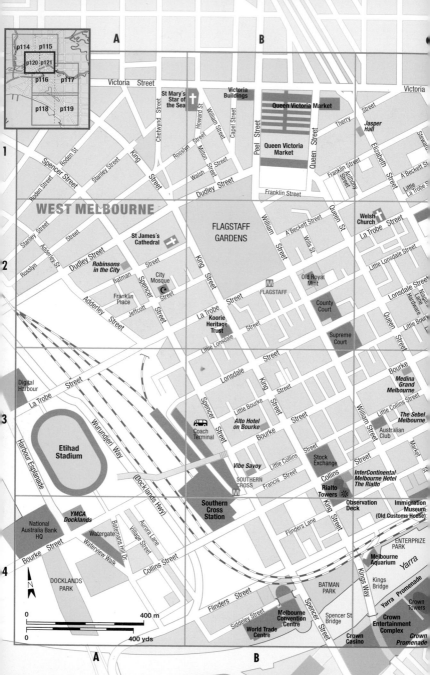

Victoria Street

St Mary's Star of the Sea

Victoria Buildings

Queen Victoria Market

Queen Victoria Market

Jasper Hall

Victoria Street

WEST MELBOURNE

Chetwynd Street

Howard St

William Street

Capel Street

Peel Street

Therry Street

Queen Street

Franklin Street

Anthony Street

Elizabeth Street

Stewart Street

A Beckett Street

Little La Trobe St

Roden St

Spencer Street

Stanley Street

King Street

Rosslyn Street

Milton Street

Walsh Street

Dudley Street

Franklin Street

Stanley Street

Adderley St

Rosslyn Street

Dudley Street

Batman Street

St James's Cathedral

Robinsons in the City

City Mosque

FLAGSTAFF GARDENS

William Street

A Beckett Street

Willis St

Welsh Church

La Trobe Street

Little Lonsdale Street

Lonsdale Street

Franklin Place

Jeffcott Street

Spencer Street

King Street

La Trobe Street

Koorie Heritage Trust

Old Royal Mint

County Court

Supreme Court

Queen St

Niagara Hardware

Little Bourke St

Queen Street

Adderley Street

Street

Little Lonsdale Street

Lonsdale Street

King Street

Bourke Street

Medina Grand Melbourne

Digital Harbour

La Trobe Street

Wurundjeri Way

(Docklands Hwy)

Spencer Street

Little Bourke Street

Bourke Street

Street

William Street

Little Collins Street

The Sebel Melbourne

Australian Club

Market Street

Etihad Stadium

Harbour Esplanade

Coach Terminal

Alto Hotel on Bourke

Vibe Savoy

Little Collins Street

Francis Street

Stock Exchange

Collins Street

SOUTHERN CROSS

InterContinental Melbourne Hotel The Rialto

Rialto Towers

YMCA Docklands

National Australia Bank HQ

Watergardens

Waterview Walk

Batmans Hill Dr

Aurora Lane

Village Street

Collins Street

Southern Cross Station

King Street

Observation Deck

Immigration Museum (Old Customs House)

Flinders Lane

ENTERPRIZE PARK

Melbourne Aquarium

Yarra

Bourke Street

DOCKLANDS PARK

Flinders Street

Siddeley Street

Melbourne Convention Centre

Spencer Street

BATMAN PARK

Spencer St Bridge

Kings Way

Kings Bridge

Yarra Promenade

Crown Towers

N

0   400 m

0   400 yds

World Trade Centre

Crown Casino

Crown Entertainment Complex

Crown Promenade

Yarra Promenade

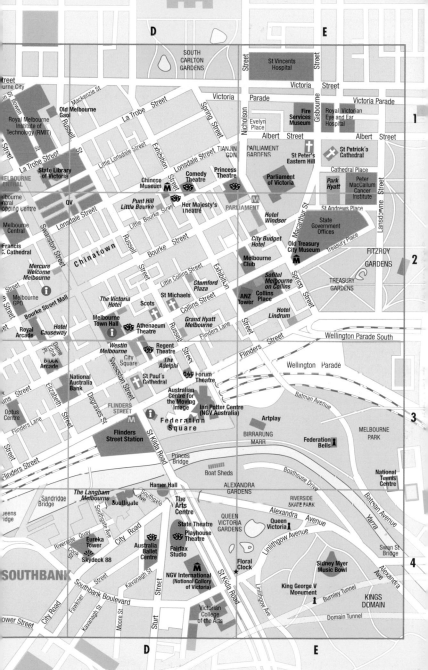

Street Index

Index

Bars and Pubs

Insight Smart Guide: Melbourne
Compiled by: **Amy Van**
Edited by: **Sarah Sweeney**
Proofread and indexed by: **Neil Titman**

Photography by: **Aylyx** 75; **Corbis** 46, 59, 70; Courtesy **Cumberland Lorne** 67; **APA Jerry Dennis** 2/T, 3M/ML/MR/T, 4B, 5, 7/T, 8, 9/T, 10, 11, 14, 16, 17T, 18, 19B, 21T, 22, 23B, 25/T, 26/27, 28, 29, 30T, 31, 32, 34, 38, 39, 40, 41T, 43T, 44, 48, 49/T, 51, 53/T, 55, 57, 65, 68, 69T, 73, 77/T, 79, 83B, 87T, 89, 95, 97, 98, 100, 101, 103, 107, 108, 109/T, 110, 111/T; **Downtowner** 64; **Mary Evans** 58; Courtesy **Fifteen London** 88; **Fotolia** 24; Courtesy **George Lane Bar** 35; Courtesy **Glass House Hotel** 57T; **John Gollings** 3BL; Courtesy **Hellenic Republic** 92T; Courtesy **Immigration Museum** 76; Courtesy **Hotel jasper** 61B; **Kobal** 51; Courtesy **Laird Hotel** 56; Courtesy **the Langham** 65T; **Leonardo** 67; Courtesy **Longrain** 89B; **Los Cardinos** 74; Courtesy **Melbourne Symphony Orchestra** 82; **MTC Theatre** 105B; Courtesy **National Sport Museum** 78; **NGV International** 80B; Courtesy **The Prince** 66; **Rex Features** 50; Courtesy **Rockpool Bar and Grill** 93; **David Simmonds** 6; Courtesy **Softitel Melbourne** 63; **Stamford Plaza** 62; APA **Victoria Starr** 3BR, 4T, 12, 13/T, 15, 17B, 19T, 20, 21B, 30, 33/T, 36, 37/T, 41B, 42, 43, 45, 47/T, 52, 54, 60, 69, 71, 72, 80T, 81, 83, 84, 85, 86, 87, 92, 96, 99/T, 101B, 102, 1904, 105, 106,

107T, 112/113; Courtesy **Stokehouse** 94; Courtesy **Taxi Dining Room** 91; Visions of Victoria 71T; Courtesy **Hotel Windsor** 61
Cover pictures by: **Getty Images** (front) **photolibrary.com** (back)

Picture Manager: **Steven Lawrence**
Maps: **Stephen Ramsay and APA Cartography Department**
Series Editor: **Sarah Sweeney**

First Edition 2011
©2011 Apa Publications (UK) Limited

Printed by CTPS-China

Worldwide distribution enquiries:
APA Publications GmbH & Co Verlag KG (Singapore branch)
7030 Ang Mo Kio Ave 5
08-65 Northstar @ AMK
Singapore 569880
email: apasin@signet.com.sg

Distributed in the UK and Ireland by:
GeoCenter International Ltd
Meridian House,
Churchill Way West,
Basingstoke,
Hampshire, RG21 6YR;
tel: (44 1256) 817 987;
email: sales@geocenter.co.uk

Distributed in the United States by:
Ingram Publisher Services
One Ingram Blvd, PO Box 3006

La Vergne, TN 37086-1986
email: customer.service@ingrampublisher
services.com

Distributed in Australia by:
Universal Publishers
PO Box 307
St. Leonards, NSW 1590
tel: (02) 9857 3700
email: sales@universalpublishers.com.au

Distributed in New Zealand by:
Hema Maps New Zealand Ltd (HNZ),
Unit 2, 10 Cryers Road,
East Tamaki, Auckland 2013;
tel: (64) 9-273 6459;
email: sales.hema@clear.net.nz

Contacting the Editors
We would appreciate it if readers would alert us to errors or outdated information by writing to:
Apa Publications, PO Box 7910, London SE1 1WE, UK; fax: (44 20) 7403 0290;
email: insight@apaguide.co.uk

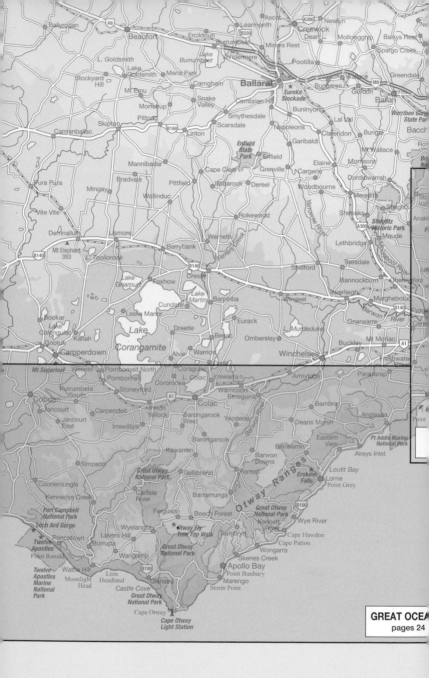

GREAT OCEAN
pages 24